JN116270

The True-to-life Image of Nichiren Daishonin
(Kagami-no-miei, stored at Head Temple Taisekiji)

THE LIFE OF NICHIREN DAISHONIN

日蓮大聖人の御生涯

Nichiren Shoshu
Commemorative Committee
for the 800th Anniversary of the Advent of the Founder Nichiren Daishonin

THE LIFE OF NICHIREN DAISHONIN

CONTENTS

2. The Establishment of True Buddhism

3. Propagation in Kamakura

4. The Sado Period

6. Nichiren Daishonin's Passing

Appendices

FOREWORD

It is my greatest pleasure to publish *The Life of Nichiren Daishonin* on the occasion of commemorating the 800th anniversary of the advent of our Founder, Nichiren Daishonin.

The biographical writings of Nichiren Daishonin have been published in large numbers from various quarters including the other Buddhist sects. But, many of them do not correctly understand the Daishonin, and in most cases they describe the Daishonin merely as a bodhisattva who propagated the Lotus Sutra after many years of hardships and sufferings.

It is truly meaningful for the Overseas Department of Nichiren Shoshu to present *The Life of Nichiren Daishonin* so that our founder Nichiren Daishonin will be correctly recognized as the True Buddha in the Latter Day of the Law, for eternity.

The advent of Nichiren Daishonin in the Latter Day of the Law meets the Buddha's prophesy, and the purpose of his advent is to lead each and every one of those without the seed of Buddhahood to enlightenment.

In the Gosho, *Letter to Jakunichi-bo* (Jakunichi bo-gosho), it is taught as follows:

> The sutra states, "Just as the sunlight or the moonlight dispels the darkness, this person will practice [Myoho-Renge-Kyo] in the world and eliminate [the fundamental] darkness of all living beings." Carefully ponder on the meaning of these words.

"This person will practice [Myoho-Renge-Kyo] in the world" means that Bodhisattva Jogyo makes his advent in the first five hundred years of the Latter Day of the Law, reveals the light of the five characters of Nam-Myoho-Renge-Kyo, and illuminates the fundamental darkness and the darkness of earthly desires.

(*Gosho*, p. 1393)

The Daishonin made his advent in the Latter Day of the Law as the reincarnation of Bodhisattva Jogyo (Superior Practice). His status as Bodhisattva Jogyo, however, is a provisional identity in every regard. From the standpoint of the profound mystery of his inner realization, the Daishonin is the reincarnation of the Buddha with the property of intrinsically perfect wisdom from the infinite past of *kuon-ganjo*.

The Twenty-sixth High Priest Nichikan Shonin stated the following in his writing, *The Meaning Hidden in the Depths* (Montei hichin-sho):

From the superficial perspective of his external status, he is Nichiren, the reincarnation of Bodhisattva Jogyo. Based on the profound mystery of his inner realization, he is Nichiren, the reincarnation of the Buddha with the property of perfect wisdom. Thus, you should understand that his original identity is the Buddha with the property of perfect wisdom, his provisional identity is Bodhisattva Jogyo, and his true identity is Nichiren.

(*Six-Volume Writings*, p. 49)

Thus, it is most essential that we, the priesthood and laity of

Nichiren Shoshu, revere our Founder Nichiren Daishonin as the True Buddha in the Latter Day of the Law, and unite in the spirit of many in body, one in mind, strictly following his teaching. Furthermore, we must devote ourselves to propagate Myoho-Renge-Kyo in order to achieve true world peace and the happiness of all mankind.

I would like to conclude my foreword by sincerely praying that all of you will read this book which was just issued, and make further efforts in your practice for yourself and others.

Nichinyo Hayase
The Sixty-eighth High Priest of Nichiren Shoshu

February 16, 2021

Editorial Preface

In conjunction with the 800th anniversary of the advent of our Founder, Nichiren Daishonin, as one of the commemorative projects by our Commemorative Committee, the Nichiren Shoshu Overseas Department compiled the writings related to the life of Nichiren Daishonin based on *The Authentic Biography of Nichiren Daishonin* (Nichiren Daishonin Shoden) and *Introduction to Nichiren Shoshu* (Nichiren Shoshu Nyumon) and completed the English translation for publication.

For interpretations of the Gosho passages quoted, the Translation Committee used the Japanese version published in the *Heisei Shimpen Nichiren Daishonin Gosho*. Furthermore, the guidance and lectures by the successive High Priests were consulted in order to convey the correct meaning of the passages.

The titles of the Gosho and other literary works are rendered in English. In most cases, the Japanese titles follow in parentheses. Buddhist terminology is presented in English and rendered in lower case, with a few exceptions, such as the "Latter Day of the Law."

Although Japanese transliterations were given in the past with macrons over the long vowels, the style of using macrons was not applied in this book, in order to maintain an overall consistency.

Chinese proper names and titles are rendered in Pinyin, instead of the older Wade-Giles system. Thus, the old spellings of T'ien-t'ai and Miao-lo are now rendered as Tiantai and Miaole.

We will be overjoyed if this translation of the life of our Founder Nichiren Daishonin helps the English-speaking believers carry out their faith and practice, while providing an opportunity to learn about Nichiren Daishonin, the True Buddha, and his teachings.

The Commemorative Committee for the 800th Anniversary of the Advent of the Founder Nichiren Daishonin

February 16, 2021

The Life of Nichiren Daishonin

The Hoando at Head Temple Taisekiji
where the Dai-Gohonzon of the High Sanctuary
of the Essential Teaching is stored

1. Nichiren Daishonin's Birth and Entering the Priesthood

Uchiura Bay (seashore near former Kataumi)

His Birth

Nichiren Daishonin was born in a fishing village called Kataumi, located in Tojo Village in Nagasa County of Awa Province (currently Kamogawa City, Chiba Prefecture) on February 16th of the first year of Jo-o (1222). His father was Mikuni-no-taifu (Nukina Jiro) Shigetada, and his mother was Umegikunyo. He was named Zennichimaro at birth.

The Daishonin states the following about his origin:

> I, Nichiren, in this life was born poor and lowly to a Chandala[1] family.

> (*Letter to Sado* [Sado-gosho], *Gosho*, p. 580)

---

1 Chandala: The lowest social class in ancient India that made a living from killing animals or handling corpses.

> I, Nichiren, am the child of a Chandala family from Isonaka,
> Kataumi, located in Tojo Village of Awa Province.
> (*The Tripitaka Master Shan Wu Wei* [Zemmui sanzo-sho],
> *Gosho*, p. 438)

He explains that he was born into the lowest social class. These passages indicate a profound meaning in Buddhism. Shakyamuni Buddha was born in India[2] to a royal family, and his Buddhism would bring salvation only to the people living during his lifetime, and in the Former and Middle Days of the Law. Unlike Shakyamuni Buddha, Nichiren Daishonin, as the True Buddha, was born to the lowest social class, and his Buddhism will save all living beings in the Latter Day of the Law.

Omens

Before Nichiren Daishonin was born, various mystic omens[3] were seen. In later years, the Second High Priest Nikko Shonin transcribed the Daishonin's words about his birth in *On What Nikko Shonin Heard from Nichiren Daishonin about his Birth* (Ubuyu sojo no koto). This is an indispensable and important record of transmission regarding the significance of the Daishonin's birth. This record reveals that the Daishonin's mother had a mystic dream, stating that when his mother conceived the Daishonin, she said:

---

2 India: India in those days used to be a vast area of Southern Asia, including current India, Nepal, Bangladesh, and Pakistan.

3 Omens: Phenomena which occur beforehand to indicate that something very important is going to happen. For example, magnificent omens occurred before the birth and death of Buddhas.

One night, I (Nichiren Daishonin's mother) had a mystic dream. In it, I sat on Mount Hiei and washed my hands with water in the lake in Omi Province. At that time, the sun rose up from Mount Fuji and entered into my body.

(*On What Nikko Shonin Heard from Nichiren Daishonin about his Birth* [Ubuyu sojo no koto], *Gosho*, p. 1708)

This mystic dream was, indeed, a good omen, which suggested the advent of the Buddha in the Latter Day of the Law.

The Daishonin in later years writes about a mystic dream that Queen Maya had when she conceived Shakyamuni Buddha:

Queen Maya had a dream that she conceived the sun, and soon after gave birth to Prince Siddhartha. Thus, the childhood name of [Shakyamuni] Buddha is translated as Nisshu (the Sun and Seed).

(*The Selection of the Time* [Senji-sho], *Gosho*, p. 862)

From this description, we can see that the mystic dreams related to both the Daishonin and Shakyamuni Buddha were very similar.

According to a legend, a few days prior to the Daishonin's birth, blue lotus flowers suddenly appeared on the surface of the ocean and bloomed beautifully. Even today, the surrounding beach still retains the name, "Renge-ga-fuchi" (Lotus Flower above the Deep Water).

Moreover, on the day the Daishonin was born, it is said that lotus flowers bloomed in a garden pond. Also on this day, it is said that gigantic sea breams leaped out of the sea, as if to celebrate the Daishonin's birth. Even now, this area is called the "Tai-no-ura"

(Seashore of Sea Breams) where large sea breams live in the water. Still today, it is a mystery as to why sea breams, a deep-sea fish, stay in the shallow waters near the shore in this area.

Even more mystic is the fact that Shakyamuni Buddha from India entered nirvana on February 15th, whereas the Daishonin from Japan was born on February 16th. This symbolizes a mystic karmic relation, indicating that the Buddhism of maturing and harvesting of Shakyamuni Buddha will vanish in the Latter Day of the Law, while the Buddhism of sowing will emerge and be propagated by the Daishonin.

We can take these numerous, mystic, causal relations and actual phenomena as a sign of the entire universe seeking and admiring the advent of the True Buddha.

The Daishonin made his advent as the True Buddha in the Latter Day of the Law. When he was born, the Buddha nature of the mountains, rivers, grasses, and trees throughout the ten directions of the entire universe manifested auspicious omens of joy toward the location of Kataumi in Awa Province.

His Birthplace

Nichiren Daishonin was born in Kataumi as described in *Questions and Answers on the Object of Worship* (Honzon mondo-sho), which states:

> I, Nichiren, am the child of a fisherman, who lived in Kataumi, located in Tojo Village in Nagasa County of Awa Province, which corresponds to the 12th [location] of the 15 provinces in the Tokaido region [in terms of distance from

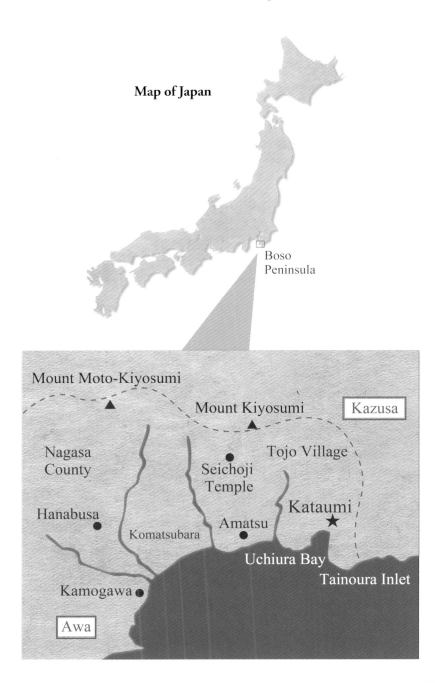

Map of Japan

Boso
Peninsula

Mount Moto-Kiyosumi

Mount Kiyosumi

Kazusa

Nagasa
County

Seichoji
Temple

Tojo Village

Hanabusa

Amatsu

Kataumi

Komatsubara

Uchiura Bay

Tainoura Inlet

Kamogawa

Awa

the capital].

(*Gosho*, p. 1279)

Kataumi is considered to correspond to current Kamogawa City in Chiba Prefecture. Nichiren Daishonin's birthplace has traditionally been considered to be "Kominato." However, the Daishonin describes his memories of the landscape around his childhood home in *Reply to Nii ama gozen* (Nii ama gozen-gohenji):

The beaches of Kataumi, Ichikawa, and Kominato...

(*Gosho*, p. 763)

Here he mentions Kataumi together with Ichikawa and Kominato. Furthermore, the existence of Kataumi, in addition to Kominato and Ichikawa, is confirmed through the local documents in this area. Therefore, Kataumi can be thought to be the name of a place or a village in the neighborhood of Kominato.

The name "Kataumi" existed until the early modern period. Over time, however, it fell out of use, and unfortunately, it is no longer possible to pinpoint its exact location.

Nevertheless, it is a fact that Kataumi was the name of a fishing village that existed at Uchiura Bay to the south of Boso Peninsula, and this is considered to be Nichiren Daishonin's birthplace. The area around Uchiura Bay overlooks the great Pacific Ocean, with the Seicho mountains rising from behind. It has a warm climate and is surrounded by scenic beauty.

Therefore, Kataumi is the perfect place where the True Buddha, who would save all living beings, was born.

The Age Defiled by the Five Impurities

Nichiren Daishonin made his advent in the first year of Jo-o (1222). This was the 2,171st year following Shakyamuni Buddha's passing, and also marked the 171st year of the Latter Day of the Law.

In the Sutra of the Great Assembly *(Daishik-kyo)*, Shakyamuni Buddha predicted the future of Buddhism:

> The first Five-hundred-year Period after my death will be the age of emancipation, and the next Five-hundred-year Period will be the age of meditation, which will add up to one thousand years. The third Five-hundred-year Period will be the age of reading, reciting, and listening, and the next Five-hundred-year Period will be the age of building temples and stupas, which will account for two thousand years. The last Five-hundred-year Period will be the age of conflict within the teachings that I have expounded. This will cause the pure Law to become obscured and lost.
>
> (*Selected Gosho Passages of Nichiren Daishonin*, p. 165)

The first thousand years after Shakyamuni's death is called the Former Day of the Law. In this period, there were people who were freed from the state of delusion and reached the state of emancipation through Shakyamuni's Buddhism.

The next thousand-year period is called the Middle Day of the Law. In this age, people respected the formalities of Buddhism and conducted recitations of the Buddhist sutras, listened to the Buddhist teachings, translated the scriptures, and built a large number of stupas and temples.

The last Five-hundred-year Period is called the Latter Day of the

Law. Shakyamuni Buddha predicted that two thousand years after his passing, the world would enter the age of conflict, the people's capacity would deteriorate, and Shakyamuni Buddha's teachings would be obscured and lost.

This prediction came true. When Nichiren Daishonin made his advent, the entire world including Japan had become defiled by the five impurities,[4] and tragedies caused by conflicts were proliferating.

In Japan it was a time of social upheaval: hierarchical relationships highly valued back in those days were destroyed, such as vassals overthrowing their lords and usurping their authority. This represents the chaotic condition of the Latter Day of the Law—the evil age defiled by the five impurities. This was clearly demonstrated by the occurrence of the unprecedented Jokyu Incident in the third year of Jokyu (1221), one year before the Daishonin's birth. During this upheaval, the Kamakura Shogunate led by Hojo Yoshitoki and others, defeated the imperial court. This resulted in the banishment of the three retired emperors—Gotoba, Tsuchimikado, and Juntoku.

In Asia around 1206, Genghis Khan declared himself as the Khan or the emperor of the Mongolian Empire, after unifying the entire land of Mongolia. Immediately after, he launched massive invasions in every direction. His powerful mounted troops instantly conquered Central Asia. Within five decades, Genghis Khan had conquered the northeastern region of China, taking possession of the northern part of the Yellow River; and the Crimean Peninsula from the coast of the Black Sea to the Ukraine region. Thus, he created the largest empire in history. His invasions were relentless, and several million people were killed.

---

4 **Five impurities:** impurity of the age, impurity of desire, impurity of living beings, impurity of view, and impurity of life, which are caused by the slander of true Buddhism. They are stated in the Expedient Means (*Hoben*; second) chapter of the Lotus Sutra.

These invasions did not cease even after the death of Genghis Khan in 1227. The Mongolian Empire vanquished various countries in Eastern Europe, including Hungary and Poland, and in the Mediterranean region from Turkey to Iran. The Mongols dominated a huge territory. The western European countries were so terrified that in 1245, the Pope sent a goodwill envoy to Mongolia as a representative of those countries. Further, in the Far East, Kublai Khan, the fifth emperor, subjugated Tibet and forced Goryeo (which corresponds to the current Korean Peninsula) to surrender. In 1271 he gave the name, Yuan to all the countries that had been conquered, and finally defeated Southern Sung in 1279, completing the unification of Chinese land under the rule of Yuan.

During the thirteenth century, the world experienced an era of invasions and mass killings. This, indeed, proves that the age of conflict predicted by Shakyamuni Buddha truly had arrived.

Kamakura Shogunate

Upon the demise of the retired Emperor Goshirakawa in the third year of Kenkyu (1192), Minamoto Yoritomo was appointed as the great general who would subdue the barbarians, a position that he long had yearned for. With this, the military rule of the Kamakura Shogunate in Japan was born in name and in reality.

For 30 some years leading up to the establishment of the shogunate, there had been continuous bloody conflict, with the strong devouring the weak. Still, this did not change even after the establishment of the shogunate.

Each time a battle occurred, the general population had to suffer from serious hardships; all they could do was to helplessly endure.

The rule of the Minamotos, who had seized power, came to an end after only three generations. Ultimately, political power fell into the hands of the Hojo clan,[5] who had served in the office of the regent. At that time, the de facto, supreme ruler was Hojo Yoshitoki, who was then acting as the regent. He reinforced his control over the manors owned by the immediate vassals of the shogun, expanding the actual power of the government.

The nobles of the imperial court saw the rights of their manors gradually taken away by the immediate vassals of the shogun, resulting in a significant diminishment of their political power and economic base.

This was a matter of life and death for the members of the aristocracy, mainly for the imperial family. After the death of the third shogun, Sanetomo, the retired Emperor Gotoba[6] determined the time was right for him to recover the power of the imperial court by taking advantage of the political strife within the government. He devised various schemes. In particular, Gotoba demanded that Yoshitoki return to him the power to appoint and remove the estate stewards, since the shogunate still held that power. Yoshitoki, however, rejected Gotoba's proposal. In fact, Yoshitoki sent his brother, Tokifusa, together with a large military display of 1,000 soldiers, to Kyoto, then the capital, to deliver his message to Gotoba. Yoshitoki also repeatedly forced a prince of Gotoba to travel from

---

5 The Hojo clan: The clan that continued to have real power in the Kamakura Shogunate during the Kamakura period from around 1192 to 1333.

6 The retired Emperor Gotoba [1180-1239]: The 82nd emperor of Japan; a fourth prince of Emperor Takakura. He became emperor in 1183 by the retired Emperor Goshirakawa's order. Although he abdicated the throne to Emperor Tsuchimikado in 1198, he ruled Japan during the reigns of Emperor Tsuchimikado, Juntoku, and Chukyo. In 1221 Emperor Gotoba issued an imperial order to subjugate Hojo Yoshitoki and took up arms against him. This is called the Jokyu Incident. However, he was defeated by Yoshitoki and banished to Oki Island, where he passed away.

Kyoto to Kamakura so that Yoshitoki could take advantage of the authority of the imperial court by having Gotoba's son assume the position of shogun. However, Gotoba also rejected this idea. In the end, there was no other choice for both parties but to settle the dispute through armed conflict.

Jokyu Incident

Finally, on May 15th in the third year of Jokyu (1221), the Imperial Court issued a command in the name of the retired Emperor Gotoba ordering that Hojo Yoshitoki and his followers be subdued; this was the beginning of the Jokyu Incident. However, the Kamakura Shogunate amassed 190,000 soldiers and completely overwhelmed the army of the retired Emperor. In only a month's time, this Jokyu Incident quickly ended with the Kamakura Shogunate's complete victory.

The Record of the Jokyu Incident (Jokyu ki) states that Kyoto was driven into a state of hell by the soldiers of the Kamakura Shogunate, who plundered it, set buildings on fire, and attacked and massacred the people there.

After the Jokyu Incident, Yoshitoki banished the retired Emperor Gotoba to Oki Island, the retired Emperor Juntoku[7] to Sado Island, and the retired Emperor Tsuchimikado[8] to Tosa Province. Moreover,

---

7 **The retired Emperor Juntoku [1197-1242]:** The 84th emperor of Japan; the third prince of Emperor Gotoba. He became emperor when his father forced Emperor Tsuchimikado to retire in 1210. In 1221, he abdicated the throne to his son, who became Emperor Chukyo, for the purpose of joining his father in the battle during the Jokyu Incident. As the army of the retired Emperor Gotoba was defeated, the retired Emperor Juntoku was banished to Sado Island, where he passed away in 1242.

8 **The retired Emperor Tsuchimikado [1195-1231]:** The 83rd emperor of Japan; the first prince of Emperor Gotoba. He became emperor in 1198 and retired in 1210. He tried to

he ordered the beheading of the main aristocrats and samurai warriors who had joined the retired Emperor Gotoba's faction opposing the shogunate.

The Jokyu Incident was unprecedented and is considered to be a watershed in Japanese history. This marked a change in the governnance structure of the Japanese government, from aristocrats and court nobles to samurai warriors, who before had been vassals of the Imperial Court. This political upheaval, with the subordinates overthrowing their superiors, represents the state in the Latter Day of the Law, defiled with the five impurities.

It was during this age of conflicts and wars when Nichiren Daishonin was born, because the True Buddha felt it was time to make his advent in this age of extreme conflict and anger. Here, we can see a profound causal relationship in this world from the Buddhist point of view.

Determination and Pursuit of Learning

When Zennichimaro was very young, there was an increasing concern about the state of society, due to tragic incidents occurring one after another, as well as serious famines caused by natural disasters, such as heavy storms and droughts. Young Zennichimaro was very bright, and he came to consider the question of what was the cause of these various misfortunes, including the Jokyu Incident. In order to resolve such confusion in society, at the age of 12, in the first year of Tempuku (1233) he decided to pursue learning

---

stop his father from subjugating the Hojo clan. Thus, he escaped from being banished by the Kamakura Shogunate, but he voluntarily requested to be banished to what is currently Kochi Prefecture. Later, he was transferred to what is currently Tokushima Prefecture, where he passed away in 1231.

in order to become "the wisest man in Japan." He then started his studies under Dozen-bo[9] at Seichoji Temple[10] near Kataumi. There, he learned general knowledge and reading and writing, focusing on Buddhist scriptures. He was tutored mainly by his seniors, Joken-bo and Gijo-bo.[11] Because of his innate talent and seeking spirit, he more and more deepened his understanding. As time progressed, the questions that he had been vaguely contemplating all along, gradually became clear in his mind.

First, during the Jokyu Incident, the emperor's side exhausted all their energy praying for the defeat of the opponent. Prayers were offered by prominent monks, such as those from the Tendai and Shingon sects, which claim to protect and keep the nation tranquil. Despite this, they suffered a crushing defeat, resulting in the banishment of the three retired emperors. Why did this happen?

Second, why is it that devoted Nembutsu believers in Awa Province showed signs of agony at the time of death, indicating that they had fallen into the evil paths?

Third, Shakyamuni Buddha's true intention must have been to expound only one fundamental teaching. However, why is it that his teaching was divided into multiple schools of thought, each of which insisted on its own superiority?

---

9 Dozen-bo [?-1276]: A priest of Seichoji Temple. Nichiren Daishonin's master when he entered the priesthood.

10 Seichoji Temple: A temple located in the area currently known as Kiyosumi, Kamogawa City of Chiba Prefecture. At this temple, Nichiren Daishonin studied in his youth, entered the priesthood, and later, gave his first sermon.

11 Joken-bo and Gijo-bo [Dates of birth and death unknown]: Two priests who were Nichiren Daishonin's seniors who mentored him at Seichoji Temple. Later, they embraced the Daishonin's Buddhism.

Entering the Priesthood and Study Travels

When Zennichimaro was sixteen years old, he entered the priesthood and changed his name to Zesho-bo Rencho. He wanted to master the essence of Buddhism and find the answers to the questions he had. He assiduously devoted himself to his daily practice and study day and night.

Rencho thoroughly read all of the scrolls of the sutras and other writings possessed by Seichoji Temple. In the spring, two years after he entered the priesthood, Rencho set out on a journey to visit various temples in Japan with the determination to further his studies. It took him as long as 14 years to complete his studies.

Later, the Daishonin stated in *Reply to Myoho bikuni* (Myoho bikuni-gohenji):

> I went to Kamakura, Kyoto, Mount Hiei, Onjoji Temple, Mount Koya, Tennoji Temple and elsewhere, mastering their respective doctrines, at temple after temple, in province after province.
>
> (*Gosho*, p. 1258)

Seeking the many Buddhist scriptures and writings, he visited Kamakura, the center of politics and finance, and historic temples, such as Enryakuji Temple on Mount Hiei, the center of Buddhism at that time.

During his long years of study, he came to the following conclusions:

First, the various sects that went against Shakyamuni Buddha's fundamental doctrines were the cause of all the disasters.

Second, the Law that should be propagated in the Latter Day of the Law is the five characters of Myoho-Renge-Kyo, which is the essence of the Lotus Sutra.

And finally, he awakened to the realization that he, himself, was the reincarnation of Bodhisattva Jogyo (Superior Practice), who will save the people in the impure age of the Latter Day of the Law, based on the five characters of Myoho-Renge-Kyo.

The Life of Nichiren Daishonin

Nichiren Daishonin's Study Travel Route

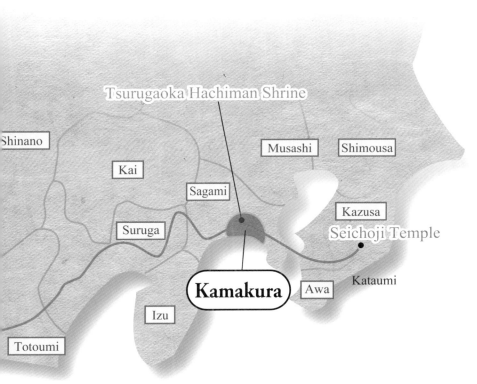

1. **Onjoji Temple**

2. **Mount Hiei (Enryakuji Temple)**

3. **Toji Temple**

4. **Sennyuji Temple**

5. **Ninnaji Temple**

6. **Shitennoji Temple**

7. **Yakushiji Temple**

8. **Mount Koya (Kongobuji Temple)**

2. The Establishment of True Buddhism

Kasagamori Forest

The Declaration of the Establishment of True Buddhism

After completing his travels for Buddhist study, Rencho returned to Seichoji Temple in his home province at the age of 32 in the spring of the fifth year of Kencho (1253). After profound consideration, he made an unshakable resolution to propagate the great Law of "Nam-Myoho-Renge-Kyo," no matter what major obstacles may appear. Before dawn on March 28th of the same year, Rencho walked up to the Kasagamori Forest, at the top of Mount Kiyosumi. There, he chanted Nam-Myoho-Renge-Kyo toward the entire universe, facing the rising sun. This was the first time when he revealed the Daimoku of his inner realization.

Right after the revelation of the Daimoku, at Seichoji Temple he began to preach his teachings, including the doctrine stating that Nembutsu leads to the hell of incessant suffering. And after one month had passed, on April 28th, he declared the establishment of true Buddhism by clearly preaching to all the people the Daimoku that he would propagate throughout his life.

Later, Nichiren Daishonin expressed his feeling as follows:

> If I speak even a word about it [that Nembutsu and other heretical teachings will lead one into the evil paths], then I will surely meet opposition from my parents, my brothers, and my masters, and I will also suffer persecution from the sovereign. If I stay silent, I will be lacking compassion. Based on the teachings of the Lotus Sutra and Nirvana Sutra, I have contemplated whether I should speak out or remain silent. These sutras expound that if I do not speak out, this life may be eventless, but undoubtedly I will fall into the hell of incessant suffering in my next lifetime. I came to realize that if I did speak out, I would encounter the three obstacles and four devils[12] without fail.
>
> (*The Opening of the Eyes* [Kaimoku-sho], *Gosho*, pp. 538-539)

The "Nam-Myoho-Renge-Kyo" that Nichiren Daishonin began to chant is the Daimoku of the unprecedented sole essential teaching that will save all living beings. This Daimoku arose from the easternmost land of Japan and will spread throughout the world during the Latter Day of the Law and into the eternal future as indicated in the following two passages:

> When I pondered the matter, based on the Buddha's prophecy described in the sutras, I came to the conclusion that the present time definitely corresponds to the beginning of the fifth Five-hundred-year Period. There is no doubt that

---

12 **Three obstacles and four devils:** Three kinds of hindrances and four kinds of evil functions that obstruct one in carrying out the Buddhist practice and lead one into the evil paths: the three obstacles of earthly desires, karma, and retribution; and the four devils of earthly desires, five components, death, and the devils of the Sixth Heaven.

Buddhism shall arise from the easternmost land of Japan.
(*On the Buddha's Prophecy* [Kembutsu mirai ki], *Gosho*, p. 678)

Since Nichiren's compassion is vast, Nam-Myoho-Renge-Kyo will prevail for ten thousand years and beyond into the future. It possesses the beneficial power to open the blind eyes of all the people in Japan, and it blocks the path to the hell of incessant suffering.
(*Repaying Debts of Gratitude* [Ho-on-sho], *Gosho*, p. 1036)

The Name "Nichiren"

When Rencho established true Buddhism, he took this opportunity to change his name to Nichiren. His name consists of the two Chinese characters "Nichi" and "Ren," which mean "Sun" and "Lotus." This derives from two passages in the Lotus Sutra.

First, the Emerging from the Earth (*Juji yujutsu*; fifteenth) chapter

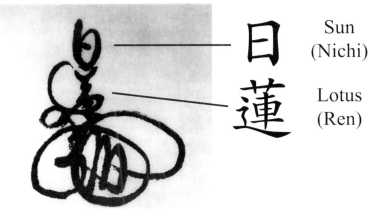

日　Sun (Nichi)

蓮　Lotus (Ren)

Nichiren Daishnon's name and signature

of the Lotus Sutra states:

> [The votary of the Lotus Sutra] is not defiled by earthly desires and slanders. This is likened to the lotus flower remaining untainted by the muddy water.
>
> (*Hokekyo*, p. 425)

Second, the Wondrous Powers of the Tathagata (*Nyorai jinriki*; twenty-first) chapter of the Lotus Sutra reads:

> Just as the sunlight or moonlight dispels the darkness, this person will practice [Myoho-Renge-Kyo] in the world and eliminate [the fundamental] darkness of all living beings.
>
> (*Hokekyo*, p. 516)

Based on the above-cited passages, the Daishonin explains his own name in *Letter to the Wife of Shijo Kingo* (Shijo kingo nyobo-gosho) as follows:

> [The benefits of this medicine] are as clear as the sun and the moon, and as pure as a lotus flower. The Lotus Sutra can be compared to the sun and the moon, and a lotus flower. This is why the sutra is named Myoho-Renge-Kyo. I, Nichiren, am also likened to the sun and the moon, and a lotus flower.
>
> (*Gosho*, p. 464)

As the Daishonin mentions, the name "Nichiren" indicates that Nichiren Daishonin is the reincarnation of Bodhisattva Jogyo, who will illuminate the fundamental darkness of all living beings during the ten thousand years of the Latter Day of the Law and into the eternal future, and purify this defiled world. His behavior can be compared to the sun that illuminates all darkness and the pristine lotus flower that blooms in muddy water from which it grows.

Furthermore, the Daishonin states in *Letter to Jakunichi-bo* (Jakunichi bo-gosho):

> I gave myself the name Nichiren on the basis of the enlightenment that I have attained by myself.
>
> (*Gosho*, p. 1393)

Hence, he proclaims that he is in the state of Buddhahood.

Significance of the Title "Daishonin"

In Nichiren Shoshu, our founder has been respectfully called "Nichiren Daishonin." This honorific title signifies that Nichiren Daishonin is the True Buddha. Originally, Nichiren Daishonin referred to this title of *dai-sho-nin* (literally means "supreme sage") as another name for "Buddha."

He states in the Gosho as follows:

> I, Nichiren, am an insignificant common mortal. However, from the standpoint of upholding the Lotus Sutra, I am the one and only supreme individual *(dai-nin)* in Japan today.
>
> (*The Selection of the Time* [Senji-sho], *Gosho*, p. 869)

> Nichiren is the unparalleled sage *(sho-nin)* in all of Jambudvipa.[13]

---

13 **Jambudvipa:** This signifies this world, the *saha* world, where humans live. According to

> (*A Sage Knows the Three Existences of Life* [Shonin chisanze ji],
> *Gosho*, p. 748)

> A Buddha, a World-Honored One, is one who speaks the truth. That is why the Buddha is referred to as the sage *(sho-nin)* and the supreme individual *(dai-nin)*. In non-Buddhist literature and teachings, the one who speaks the truth is also called a wise man, a sage, an inhabitant of heaven, or a hermit. However, since a World-Honored One is supreme and superior to them all, he is referred to as the supreme individual *(dai-nin)*.
>
> (*The Opening of the Eyes* [Kaimoku-sho], *Gosho*, p. 529)

Both *dai-nin* and *sho-nin* mentioned in the above passages indicate honorific titles of the Buddha. One who speaks the truth, who knows the three existences of life, and who reveals the true teaching is called the "Buddha" or "World-Honored One." This is because his words and behavior are supreme and most noble.

He further preaches in the Gosho as follows:

> According to the principle expounded by the true sutra, I am convinced that, when Buddhism falls into serious disorder in the Latter Day of the Law, a supreme sage *(dai-sho-nin)* will appear in this world.
>
> (*Reply to Hyoe-sakan* [Hyoe sakan dono-gohenji],
> *Gosho*, p. 1270)

> You should realize that the supreme sage *(dai-sho-nin)* resides in this country.

ancient Indian cosmology, it is located to the south of Mount Sumeru.

(Letter to Horen [Horen-sho], *Gosho,* p. 823)

These passages declare that the supreme sage *(dai-sho-nin)* will make his advent in the Latter Day of the Law. They indicate that Nichiren Daishonin will appear as the True Buddha in the Latter Day of the Law and definitely will bring salvation to all living beings in this world with the great teaching of Myoho-Renge-Kyo. Nichiren Daishonin states:

> I came to the conclusion that the present time definitely corresponds to the beginning of the fifth Five-hundred-year Period. There is no doubt that Buddhism shall arise from the easternmost land of Japan...You should know that [now is the time when] the sage who is equal to the Buddha will be born.
> *(On the Buddha's Prophecy* [Kembutsu mirai ki], *Gosho,* p. 678)

Since Nichiren Shoshu follows the teaching of Nichiren Daishonin, we use the title, *dai,* because he is the supreme individual in all of Jambudvipa. Moreover, combining the honorific titles *dai-nin* and *sho-nin,* we respectfully designate him as the *dai-sho-nin,* and revere him as the True Buddha in the Latter Day of the Law.

The followers of other Nichiren sects call him "Most Reverend Nichiren" or "Great Bodhisattva Nichiren." However, in the Gosho, the Daishonin gives the following admonishment:

> Even if the people of the nation pay heed to Nichiren, the country will fall into ruin if they do not properly respect him.
> *(On the Buddha's Behavior* [Shuju onfurumai-gosho],
> *Gosho,* p. 1066)

Since the various other Nichiren sects have not received the transmission of the Heritage of the Law, they cannot understand and believe in Nichiren Daishonin as the True Buddha in the Latter Day of the Law. Thus, they are the ones who are being disrespectful to the True Buddha and are slandering the true Law.

The First Sermon of Nichiren Daishonin

On April 28th, at the hour of the Horse (noon), Nichiren Daishonin ascended to the dais in the Jibutsudo hall[14] of the Shobutsubo[15] at Seichoji Temple. There, he began his propagation of Nam-Myoho-Renge-Kyo. The Daishonin stated that the Lotus Sutra was the supreme of all the Buddhist teachings. Furthermore, he declared that all living beings in the Latter Day of the Law could be saved only by Nam-Myoho-Renge-Kyo. Moreover, he proclaimed that holding attachments to other teachings is a serious error.

When Tojo Kagenobu,[16] the feudal lord of the area around Seichoji Temple, listened to the Daishonin's preaching, he became furious because he was a fanatic believer of Nembutsu. He immediately tried to assault the Daishonin. This was actual proof of the passage in the

---

14 Jibutsudo hall: A hall built on the grounds of a temple or on the premises of a lay believer's house where objects of worship are enshrined.

15 Shobutsubo: One of the temples belonging to Seichoji Temple on Mount Kiyosumi, where Nichiren Daishonin entered the priesthood and studied. He preached the teaching of Nam-Myoho-Renge-Kyo for the first time to the people who gathered in the Jibutsudo hall of Shobutsubo Temple.

16 Tojo Kagenobu [?-1264]: The feudal lord of Tojo Village in Nagasa County of Awa Province. He continued to persecute the Daishonin from the first day Nichiren Daishonin preached the teaching of Nam-Myoho-Renge-Kyo. On November 11th of the first year of Bunnei (1264), together with a few hundred soldiers, Kagenobu assaulted the Daishonin and his followers at Komatsubara (Komatsubara Persecution). Soon after this, Kagenobu died in agony.

Encouraging Devotion (*Kanji*; thirteenth) chapter of the Lotus Sutra, which states:

> Many arrogant people will speak ill of and curse [the votary of the Lotus Sutra], while others will assault him with swords and staves.
>
> (*Hokekyo*, p. 375)

Nichiren Daishonin, however, managed to escape with the assistance of Joken-bo and Gijo-bo. He stayed awhile in Hanabusa, which was outside of Kagenobu's feudal domain.

Guiding Nichiren Daishonin's Parents to True Buddhism

After escaping the attack by Tojo Kagenobu and his followers, the Daishonin went to visit his parents. He decided that the time had come to truly fulfill his filial duties and repay his debt of gratitude to them. At first, they worried about the incident at his first sermon, when he lectured on his teaching at Seichoji Temple. The Daishonin described the situation in the Gosho:

> My parents beseeched me and tried to stop me.
>
> (*On Rajagrha* [Oshajo ji], *Gosho*, p. 976)

The Daishonin's parents were concerned about him and begged him to change his determination, go back to Dozen-bo, and spend his life as a priest of Seichoji Temple.

However, the Daishonin earnestly explained his doctrines to them in detail: among all the sutras, the Lotus Sutra is indeed, the ultimate purpose of the advent of various Buddhas of the three existences, and it is the direct path to attain enlightenment.

As they listened to his well-reasoned teaching and faced the venerable appearance of the Daishonin, they found themselves putting their palms together. Finally, they determined to discard their faith in the Nembutsu teaching, uphold faith in the Lotus Sutra, and chant the Daimoku. Upon their taking faith in true Buddhism, the Daishonin gave the Buddhist name "Myonichi" to his father, and "Myoren" to his mother. Both of these names included one Chinese character from the Daishonin's name, "Nichiren." Thus, he achieved his determination to lead his parents to the true teaching. This was the utmost filial duty and the true way to repay his debt of gratitude to them.

Afterwards, the Daishonin left Awa, his place of birth, and headed toward Kamakura, which was the center of government and politics at the time. From there, with the light of Myoho-Renge-Kyo, he started this journey to illuminate the world, where evil teachings and corruption were rampant, in order to save all living beings in the Latter Day of the Law and on into eternity.

3. Propagation in Kamakura

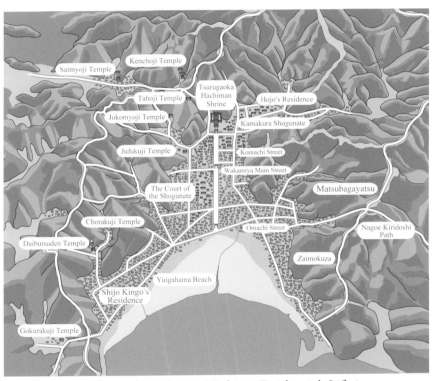

Map of Kamakura during Nichiren Daishonin's Lifetime

A Hut in Matsubagayatsu

It is said that with a firm determination to propagate the true Law, the Daishonin traveled from his hometown, Kataumi, to Izumiya (currently known as Namuya) via the western beaches of Awa Province. He then traveled by boat from Izumiya to Yonegahama Beach (currently known as Yokosuka) on the Miura Peninsula, and finally reached Kamakura via Miura Road.

The Daishonin was convinced that Kamakura was the singular place to engage in propagation activities, since it was the capital of the military government, the center of commerce, and a city crowded with large temples of various Buddhist sects, which were thriving at the time. It was inevitable that once the Daishonin propagated his Buddhist doctrines there, many persecutions should follow.

Around August of the fifth year of Kencho (1253), soon after he took up residence in Kamakura, the Daishonin built a small hut in a place called Matsubagayatsu in Nagoe. For the next 18 years, this dwelling served as his propagation center, up to the time of the Tatsunokuchi Persecution, which took place in the eighth year of Bunnei (1271).

Street Preaching

A passage in the Gosho, *On Refuting Ryokan and Others* (Ha ryokan to-gosho) reads:

> As I stated before, in the spring of the fifth year of Kencho (1253), at the age of 32, I started to refute the Nembutsu sect, the Zen sect, and others…
>
> (*Gosho*, p. 1078)

As described in this Gosho, soon after the Daishonin arrived in Kamakura, he stood in the streets, and dauntlessly refuted erroneous teachings and revealed the truth. He did so in a dignified manner, declaring "Nembutsu leads to the hell of incessant suffering," and "Zen is the teaching of devils." This was the beginning of his "street preaching."

Since the Daishonin was completely unknown to the people in Kamakura during those early days, he first needed to carry out street preaching to the people who passed by, in order to propagate a totally new teaching in Kamakura.

At present, in Kamakura there are several places, which are said to be the historic sites of the Daishonin's street preaching. Among these locations, the site of Komachi is well known. It is one street east of Wakamiya Main Street. This is where the shogunate was located,

with its family quarters and the regent's residence just to the north. Komachi was as busy as other areas, such as Omachi, Komemachi, and Okura, where the market was open on a regular basis. Komachi also was relatively close to the Daishonin's hut in Matsubagayatsu.

There also was a place called Hikigayatsu, located between Matsubagayatsu and Komachi, where Hiki Yoshimoto (Daigaku Saburo)[17] once lived. This individual later converted to the Daishonin's Buddhism, together with his wife.

In *Letter to Nakaoki nyudo* (Nakaoki nyudo-goshosoku), the Daishonin states:

> At first, only I, Nichiren, chanted the Daimoku. Since then, those who saw me, encountered me, or heard me, covered their ears, glared in fury, contorted their mouths, clenched

---

17 Hiki Yoshimoto [1202-1286]: His full name was Hiki Daigaku Saburo Yoshimoto. One of the Daishonin's lay believers who lived during the Daishonin's lifetime. He was a scholar officer of the Kamakura Shogunate specializing in Confucianism. It is said that the Daishonin asked him to review the *Rissho ankoku-ron* prior to his submission to the government. Through this process, Yoshimoto took faith in Nichiren Daishonin's Buddhism. He received several Gosho writings, such as *Letter to Daigaku Saburo* (Daigaku saburo dono-gosho), from the Daishonin.

their fists, and ground their teeth. Even my parents, brothers, masters, and good friends all became my enemies.

(*Gosho*, pp. 1431-1432)

The expression "those who saw me, encountered me, or heard me" also indicates that the Daishonin widely and actively propagated his teachings to the people in Kamakura.

From these points, we can conclude that street preaching was the Daishonin's first step in propagating Nam-Myoho-Renge-Kyo and refuting the teachings of various Buddhist sects, which are the cause of calamities and disasters.

As more disciples, such as Nissho[18] and Nichiro,[19] and lay believers, such as Toki Jonin[20] and Shijo Yorimoto[21] took faith, the Daishonin gradually started to use other means of propagation, such as dialogues and discussions.

---

18 Nissho [1221-1323]: One of the six senior priests appointed by Nichiren Daishonin from among his disciples. Also called Ben-ko or Ben Ajari. He became a disciple of the Daishonin in 1254. After the Daishonin's passing, he called himself a priest of the Tendai sect and turned his back on Nikko Shonin.

19 Nichiro [1245-1320]: One of the six senior priests of Nichiren Daishonin's disciples. Also called Chikugo-bo or Daikoku Ajari. After the Daishonin's passing, Nichiro, going against his master's will, took a statue of Shakyamuni Buddha from the Daishonin's grave site.

20 Toki Jonin [1216-1299]: Also called Toki nyudo. One of the influential believers, together with Ota Jomyo and Soya Kyoshin, who lived in the area which corresponds to current Chiba Prefecture. He received many Gosho writings from Nichiren Daishonin, such as *The True Object of Worship* (Kanjin no honzon-sho).

21 Shijo Yorimoto [1229-1296]: Shijo nakatsukasa saemon-no-jo Yorimoto. Also called Shijo Kingo. One of the powerful followers during Nichiren Daishonin's lifetime. A samurai warrior in Kamakura who served Ema Mitsutoki, a member of the Hojo clan. He took faith in Nichiren Daishonin's Buddhism soon after the Daishonin declared the establishment of true Buddhism in 1253. At the time of the Tatsunokuchi Persecution in 1271, he followed the Daishonin to the execution site, determined to die with him if the Daishonin were to be beheaded. He was also skilled in medicine, and treated Ema Mitsutoki as well as the Daishonin when each of them became ill. He received many Gosho writings, such as *The Opening of the Eyes* (Kaimoku-sho).

The initial focus of the Daishonin's propagation efforts was on refuting the Nembutsu sect, which had widely prevailed among the people at that time. The Gosho, *Letter to Akimoto* (Akimoto-gosho) states as follows:

> Although there are many people and provinces in Japan, everyone in unison chants Namu-Amida-Butsu. They revere Amida Buddha as the object of worship; they pray for rebirth in the pure land in the west and disdain the remaining nine directions.
>
> Everyone, including those who practice the Lotus Sutra, those who embrace the Shingon teachings, those who uphold the precepts, and the wise and the foolish, believes that chanting the Nembutsu is the primary practice. Thus, even as they practice their own teachings, they chant the name of Amida Buddha as a superior means to eradicate their negative karma.
>
> (*Gosho*, p. 1448)

The First Remonstration with the Nation

During the Kencho, Kogen, and Shoka eras, which correspond to the mid-Kamakura periods, there was a succession of unprecedented, abnormal incidents and tragic disasters, such as destructive fires, raging rainstorms, great earthquakes, and epidemics. In response to these, the government ordered each religious sect to pray for the elimination of the disasters, but their prayers were in vain. In particular, a major earthquake occurred on a scale that had never happened before on August 23rd of the first year of Shoka (1257). In order to locate the sutras clarifying the cause of these misfortunes, the Daishonin went into the sutra storehouse of Jissoji Temple in Iwamoto of Suruga Province (what is currently known as Fuji City of Shizuoka Prefecture) and started to peruse all the sutras, in February of the following year. The 13-year-old Hoki-ko (later called Nikko Shonin) met the Daishonin when he was carrying out practices at the nearby Shijuku-in Temple. He was so inspired by the Daishonin's venerable personality and noble figure that he decided to become his

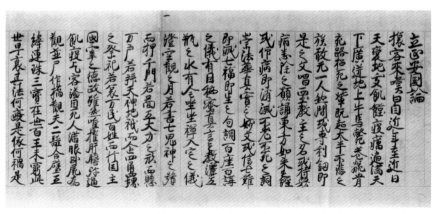

The *Rissho ankoku-ron*, handwritten by Nichiren Daishonin
(stored at Nakayama Hokekyoji Temple of Nichiren-shu sect)

disciple and began to serve him.

In the first year of Bunno (1260), the Daishonin completed the remonstration document called the *Rissho ankoku-ron* (On Securing the Peace of the Land through the Propagation of True Buddhism), which is the most important writing of his life. On July 16th of the same year, he sent this writing to the most influential man in Japan, Hojo Tokiyori [22] via Yadoya nyudo.[23]

There is a passage in the document that states:

> I find that all people have gone against the correct Law and become wholly devoted to evil doctrines. This is why all the guardian deities have abandoned this country and sages have left this land, not to return. Seizing this opportunity, devils and demons rush in, bringing disasters and calamities.
>
> (*Gosho*, p. 234)

In this passage, he points out the causal relationship of all the unprecedented disasters. In other words:

> All the people have slandered the correct Law and followed heretical teachings.
>
> It has caused the guardian deities, who no longer can enjoy the flavor of the correct Law, to abandon the country.
>
> Instead, devils and demons have rushed in to take over the temples and shrines.

---

22 Hojo Tokiyori [1227-1263]: The fifth regent of the Kamakura Shogunate. After retiring as the regent, he established Saimyoji Temple, entered the priesthood, and resided there; this is why he was referred to as Saimyoji.

23 Yadoya nyudo [Dates of birth and death unknown]: Yadoya Mitsunori. A vassal to Hojo Tokiyori and Tokimune, both regents of the Kamakura Shogunate. Yadoya Mitsunori was a close aide to Hojo Tokiyori.

This is the reason why such unprecedented disasters have repeatedly occurred.

He concludes in the *Rissho ankoku-ron* that it is essential to renounce the erroneous doctrine of Nembutsu, which was most prevalent at that time, and to convert solely to the Lotus Sutra, the only true Law.

He further predicted that two kinds of disasters would occur if the ruler of the country did not eradicate slanders and did not listen to the golden words of the Buddha. These two disasters that had not yet occurred are the disasters of revolt within one's domain and invasion from foreign lands, two of the seven described in the Sutra of the Medicine Master *(Yakushi-kyo)*, the Sutra of the Benevolent King *(Ninno-kyo)*, and so forth.

Thus, the Daishonin remonstrated with the government by submitting the *Rissho ankoku-ron* to correct the people's erroneous idea of devoting themselves to heretical doctrines. This was his first remonstration with the ruler of the nation.

The Daishonin asked Yadoya nyudo to forward the *Rissho ankoku-ron* to Hojo Tokiyori and to convey the following words:

> You must renounce the Zen and Nembutsu sects.
> (*The Selection of the Time* [Senji-sho], *Gosho*, p. 867)

In this way, the Daishonin refuted not only the Nembutsu but also the Zen sect, which Hojo Tokiyori revered.

Matsubagayatsu Persecution

The government administrators, who were staunch followers of the popular Buddhist sects at the time, not only rejected the *Rissho ankoku-ron*, but also resented Nichiren Daishonin and secretly devised an evil plot against him.

With the consent of Hojo Shigetoki (also known as Gokurakuji nyudo and the father of the regent of the Kamakura government at that time), a group of slanderous people, including many Nembutsu believers, attacked the Daishonin in his Matsubagayatsu hut in the middle of the night. This occurred on August 27th of the first year of Bunno (1260).

The Daishonin, however, mysteriously escaped from this life-threatening attack without even a single injury.

The Daishonin stated the following regarding this persecution:

> In the middle of the night, a few thousand surged to my small hut in an attempt to kill me. But how mysterious! I somehow again survived that night.
> (*Letter to Shimoyama* [Shimoyama-goshosoku],
> *Gosho*, p. 1150)

After that, the Daishonin stayed at the residence of Toki Jonin, located in Shimousa Province, (present Chiba Prefecture) for a while. During his stay, the Daishonin led Ota Jomyo,[24] Soya Kyoshin[25] and others to take faith in his teachings through his propagation efforts in the region.

Izu Exile

In the spring of the first year of Kocho (1261), the year following the Matsubagayatsu Persecution, Nichiren Daishonin returned to Kamakura and resumed his propagation activities.

On May 12th of the same year, Hojo Nagatoki, the regent of the Kamakura government, who heard about the Daishonin's further propagation, had the Daishonin arrested. Without any questioning or investigation, Nagatoki, through the power of his authority, exiled the Daishonin

---

24 **Ota Jomyo [1222-1283]:** Also called Ota nyudo or Ota saemon-no-jo. One of the influential believers, together with Toki Jonin and Soya Kyoshin, who lived in what is currently Chiba Prefecture. He received many Gosho writings from Nichiren Daishonin, such as *On the Transmission of the Three Great Secret Laws* (Sandai hiho bonjo ji), one of the most important Goshos.

25 **Soya Kyoshin [1224-1291]:** Soya Jiro hyoe-no-jo Kyoshin. Also called Horen or Soya nyudo. One of the influential believers during the Daishonin's days, living in what is currently Ichikawa City of Chiba Prefecture. He received many Gosho writings, such as *Letter to Soya nyudo* (Soya nyudo dono-motogosho).

to Kawana of Izu (present Shizuoka Prefecture).

During his exile on Izu, the Daishonin stated:

> From the twelfth day of the fifth month of last year (1261) to the sixteenth day of the first month of this year (1262), for about two hundred and forty days, I have been devoting myself to the practice of the Lotus Sutra, day and night. This is because I have been exiled for the sake of the Lotus Sutra. I do nothing but recite and practice the sutra each and every moment. There could be no other joy greater than this for someone born as a human.
>
> (*The Four Debts of Gratitude* [Shion-sho], *Gosho*, p. 266)

This means that the Daishonin, by himself, demonstrated what was preached in the Lotus Sutra, and he expressed his joy for being able to practice according to the Buddha's teachings.

Meanwhile, upon hearing the news of the Daishonin's exile, Nikko Shonin rushed to see the Daishonin and faithfully and constantly served his master. At the same time, he assiduously performed shakubuku, through which he led Kongo-in Gyoman, a priest of the Shingon sect in Atami, and many others in the surrounding areas of Ito to convert to the Daishonin's teachings. (Both Atami and Ito are currently in Shizuoka Prefecture.)

During this period of exile, the Daishonin wrote many Goshos, including *The Four Debts of Gratitude* (Shion-sho), *On the Teaching, Capacity, Time, and Country* (Kyo ki ji koku-sho) and *On Revealing Slander* (Ken hobo-sho).

Komatsubara Persecution

In February of the third year of Kocho (1263), after receiving a letter of pardon from Hojo Tokiyori, the Daishonin returned to his lodging in Kamakura. The following autumn, the first year of Bunnei (1264), the Daishonin hurried home to Awa Province for the first time in twelve years after hearing the news that his mother, Myoren, was critically ill.

When the Daishonin arrived home, he found his mother suffering from a serious illness and her death seemed inevitable. However, through the Daishonin's prayers, his mother not only recovered, but also prolonged her life. The Daishonin mentions this event in the Gosho:

> As I, Nichiren, sincerely prayed for my compassionate mother's recovery, not only was she cured of her illness, but also her life was extended by four years.
>
> (*On Immutable and Mutable Karma* [Kaenjogo-gosho], *Gosho*, p. 760)

Afterwards, the Daishonin stayed on in Awa, devoting himself to propagating true Buddhism. Kudo Yoshitaka,[26] the feudal lord of Amatsu in Awa Province (currently Kamogawa City, Chiba Prefecture) who was a staunch believer, invited the Daishonin to his residence when he learned that the Daishonin had returned to Awa. On November 11th, the Daishonin accepted his request and

---

26 **Kudo Yoshitaka [?-1264]:** Kudo sakon-no-jo Yoshitaka. One of the Daishonin's lay believers during the Daishonin's lifetime. He was the feudal lord of Amatsu in Awa Province. At the Komatsubara Persecution, he protected Nichiren Daishonin from the attack launched by Tojo Kagenobu and his soldiers, and was killed by them. He was given the Gosho, *The Four Debts of Gratitude* (Shion-sho) by the Daishonin.

departed for Yoshitaka's residence, accompanied by approximately ten companions.

Tojo Kagenobu, the steward of Tojo Village in Nagasa County who viewed the Daishonin as an enemy of the Nembutsu sect, found out that the Daishonin was on his way to Yoshitaka's manor. At twilight, when the Daishonin and his followers were nearing Komatsubara (currently, Kamogawa City in Chiba Prefecture), Kagenobu and his men attacked the Daishonin and his party.

Komatsubara

Nichiren Daishonin describes this incident as follows:

On the eleventh day of the eleventh month, on the main street called Matsubara, in Tojo in Awa Province, between the hours of the monkey and the rooster, several hundred Nembutsu believers ambushed me. At that time, I, Nichiren, was accompanied by approximately ten people, out of whom only three or four were able to fight. The arrows poured down on our heads like rain. The slashing swords were as fierce as lightning. One of my disciples was killed in battle while two other followers were severely wounded. [Although] I was cut by a sword and sustained a beating...

(*Reply to Nanjo Hyoe Shichiro* [Nanjo hyoe shichiro dono-gosho], (*Gosho*, p. 326)

As this Gosho passage shows, the Daishonin encountered this severe persecution, which nearly took his life. Kudo Yoshitaka, who tried to protect Nichiren Daishonin from the attack, eventually lost his life.

Despite Yoshitaka's efforts, the Daishonin sustained a cut on the right side of his forehead from Kagenobu's sword and his left arm was fractured. This incident corresponds exactly to the passage in the Encouraging Devotion (*Kanji*; thirteenth) chapter of the Lotus Sutra, which states that individuals who propagate the true Law in the defiled age, will be attacked by evil people with swords and staves (*Hokekyo*, p. 375).

An Official Letter from Mongolia and Nichiren Daishonin's Remonstration

In January of the fifth year of Bunnei (1268), an emissary from Mongolia made a visit to Japan and delivered a diplomatic document to the Kamakura government. This was, in fact, a threatening letter, implying that Japan should become a vassal state of the Mongolian Empire.

The occurrence of the disaster of "invasion from foreign lands" already had been predicted in the *Rissho ankoku-ron*, written by Nichiren Daishonin eight years earlier. Now, it was about to happen in reality.

On April fifth in the same year, Nichiren Daishonin heard the news that the government had received a threatening letter from Mongolia. He then wrote *Rationale for the Submission of the Rissho ankoku-ron* (Ankokuron gokan-yurai) and sent it to a government official, Priest Hokan. He also sent two letters to Yadoya nyudo, one in August and another in September, to remonstrate again with the government. However, the Daishonin did not receive any responses.

Then, on October 11th, he sent a document to eleven individuals: to two leaders of the Kamakura government—Hojo Tokimune and Hei-no saemon-no-jo Yoritsuna,[27] two government officials—Hojo Yagenta[28] and Yadoya nyudo, and to the representatives of seven major temples—Ryokan[29] of Gokurakuji Temple, Doryu of Kenchoji Temple, a representative of the Daibutsuden, Jufukuji Temple, Jokomyoji Temple, Tahoji Temple, and Chorakuji Temple. In the letter, he requested that right and wrong should be judged through a public religious debate. He further demanded that the defeated side should immediately discard their erroneous belief and take faith in the true teaching. The reason why the Daishonin wrote these letters is stated as follows:

> It is not that I look down upon the various sects. My only desire is the peace and security of this nation.
>
> (*Letter to Chorakuji Temple* [Chorakuji eno-onjo], *Gosho*, p. 380)

---

27 Hei-no saemon-no-jo Yoritsuna [?-1293]: Taira-no Yoritsuna. He served two successive regents of the Kamakura shogunate, Hojo Tokimune and Sadatoki. As deputy chief of the Hojo clan, he wielded power in the Kamakura government. In the eighth year of Bunnei (1271), he masterminded the attack at the Matsubagayatsu hut where Nichiren Daishonin resided, and plotted to have the Daishonin beheaded at Tatsunokuchi. In the second year of Koan (1279), he started the Atsuwara Persecution. Years later, Yoritsuna and his son were executed due to an allegation that they had plotted a rebellion against the Hojo clan. This caused Yoritsuna's entire clan to perish.

28 Hojo Yagenta [Dates of birth and death unknown]: One of the Daishonin's believers, who lived in the area currently known as Kamakura City of Kanagawa Prefecture. After receiving a letter of remonstration from Nichiren Daishonin, he converted to the Daishonin's Buddhism and maintained his sincere faith.

29 Ryokan [1217-1303]: A priest of the Shingon-Ritsu sect. Ryokan established Gokurakuji Temple in Kamakura, and, with the full protection of the Hojo clan, wielded supreme power in Buddhist society.

Due to the circumstances of a pending attack by Mongolia, his single-minded hope before anything else was for the security of the nation and peace for the people.

However, the leaders of the Kamakura government refused to heed the Daishonin's admonishment. Rather, they insulted and scoffed at him.

Ryokan's Prayer for Rain

Beginning in May of the eighth year of Bunnei (1271), dry weather persisted, leading to a severe drought prevailing throughout Japan. After another month without rain, the Kamakura government ordered Ryokan of Gokurakuji Temple, who was revered by the people as a living Buddha, to offer a prayer for rain. Ryokan agreed to this, declaring that he would make rainfall within seven days, beginning on June 18th, to save the people.

Upon hearing of this, Nichiren Daishonin decided to take the opportunity to widely demonstrate to the public what was true and what was erroneous among the Buddhist teachings. He made the following proposal to Ryokan:

> If [Ryokan] brings rain within seven days, Nichiren will renounce the teaching that Nembutsu leads to the hell of incessant suffering. I will become a disciple of Ryokan shonin and embrace the two hundred and fifty precepts. However, if there is no rainfall, it will become obvious that Ryokan is extremely deceptive, even though he appears to adhere to those precepts…Ryokan should believe in the Lotus Sutra alone.
>
> (*Yorimoto's Petition* [Yorimoto chinjo], *Gosho*, p. 1131)

Ryokan accepted the Daishonin's challenge and, with his many disciples, single-mindedly prayed for rain. However, he could not make rain fall within the seven-day period. He asked the Daishonin to prolong the term of his prayer for rain for seven more days. He kept on praying, but no rain appeared. On the contrary, the drought became even more severe than before, and windstorms blew in the Kamakura region. As a result, Ryokan's prayer for rain brought further sufferings to the people. He suffered a crushing defeat in his challenge with the Daishonin.

Petition from Gyobin

The failure of Ryokan's prayer for rain was a disgrace not only for the Ritsu sect, but also for all the major temples in Kamakura that supported Ryokan.

Ryokan had been exposed by Nichiren Daishonin as an extremely arrogant false sage and a hypocrite. He had been defeated completely in his challenge to pray for rain. Nevertheless, he did not honor his promise to the Daishonin. On the contrary, with his hatred growing, Ryokan plotted with representatives of the major temples in Kamakura, and ordered a priest named Gyobin to hold a debate with the Daishonin.

Ryokan tried to make Gyobin confront Nichiren Daishonin probably because it was shortly after his complete defeat against the Daishonin and he did not want to expose himself for the debate.

On July eighth of the eighth year of Bunnei (1271), Gyobin sent a letter challenging the Daishonin and demanding a private discussion. Understanding their ill intentions, the Daishonin replied to his letter on the 13th of the same month:

> Regarding the several questions you have enumerated, it might be difficult to hold a private discussion with you. Therefore, I would suggest that we present a petition to the government officials. Then, the right and wrong should be judged under their supervision concerning the points that you presented. This is my greatest wish.
>
> (Reply to Gyobin [Gyobin-gohenji], Gosho, p. 472)

Ryokan's plot to entrap the Daishonin using a private debate failed. He then, together with other conspirators, finally took the last resort of submitting a slanderous complaint about the Daishonin to the court.

Their complaint, following the custom of those days, was forwarded from the court to the Daishonin with an order to file a written response. Nichiren Daishonin immediately wrote an initial document of defense, which is called, *Counter-claim against the Petition from Ryokan and Others* [Ryokan nen-a to sojo gohensatsu].

In his response, he thoroughly refuted the erroneous points in their petition, and at the same time, stated as follows:

> If heretical views are refuted and the truth is revealed, it will be just like the example of the one-eyed turtle,[30] which finally climbed into the hole of a floating [sandalwood] log.

---

30 Example of the one-eyed turtle: The story of the one-eyed turtle is a parable described in the Former Affairs of King Wonderful Adornment (*Myoshogonno honji*; twenty-seventh) chapter of the Lotus Sutra. It is extremely difficult and rare for a turtle with only one eye to find a perfectly fitting piece of driftwood that he can rest upon in the vast ocean. Likewise, it is difficult and rare for living beings to encounter the true Law. In this context, a public debate would be a golden opportunity for the Daishonin to refute heretical views and reveal the truth.

(*Counterclaim against the Petition from Ryokan and Others* [Ryokan nen-a to sojo gohensatsu], *Gosho*, p. 472)

Reacting to Nichiren Daishonin's counterclaim, Ryokan and his fellow conspirators, refusing to back down, started to maneuver behind the scenes. They spread false charges against the Daishonin to various people in power, and at the same time, they tried to curry favor with influential individuals. The Daishonin describes the way they behaved as follows:

Ryokan shonin respectfully offered a petition to the government to make an accusation [against Nichiren]. Doryu shonin of Kenchoji Temple, visited a magistrate's office on a palanquin, and knelt down at the officials' feet. Nuns who embrace the five hundred precepts used valuable silk to get their message heard by the government.

(*Reply to Myoho bikuni* [Myoho bikuni-gohenji], *Gosho*, p. 1267)

The wives and widows of the authorities, who blindly believed their words, raised their eyebrows in anger, and said:

[Nichiren] does not have to be interrogated. He should be beheaded immediately. His disciples should also be beheaded, banished to a remote island, or put in prison.

(*Repaying Debts of Gratitude* [Ho-on-sho], *Gosho*, p. 1030)

The Second Remonstration with the Nation

Due to the unjustified resentment of Ryokan and others on his side, on September tenth of the eighth year of Bunnei (1271), Nichiren Daishonin was summoned by the Kamakura government and interrogated by the Supreme Court. On this occasion, the Daishonin strictly remonstrated with the government, as recorded in *On the Buddha's Behavior* (Shuju onfurumai-gosho, *Gosho,* p. 1057). He warned that if they persecute Nichiren, the envoy of the Buddha, they surely will receive punishment from the guardian deities, and furthermore, the two disasters of revolt from within and foreign invasion certainly will occur in this country.

On September 12th, two days after the interrogation, Nichiren Daishonin sent a letter to Hei-no saemon-no-jo, urging him again to follow the Daishonin's words:

> You are the leading person in the country at this time. Why are you harming the greatest asset in the nation? You should immediately give the deepest consideration [to my remonstration], so that the foreign invaders can be repulsed.
> (*On the Day before Yesterday* [Issakujitsu-gosho],
> *Gosho*, p. 477)

These two reprimands infuriated Hei-no saemon-no-jo. Filled with rage, on the same day, he attacked the Daishonin's hut in Matsubagayatsu together with several hundred soldiers.

The method of assault was extraordinary just for arresting a single priest. The soldiers took every violent action they could, such as trampling on scrolls of Buddhist scriptures. It was especially significant that Sho-bo, the first retainer of Hei-no saemon-no-jo, snatched the scroll of the fifth volume of the Lotus Sutra from the Daishonin's robe and struck him hard on the head with it three times.

The fifth volume includes the Encouraging Devotion (*Kanji*; thirteenth) chapter of the Lotus Sutra, which predicts that one who propagates the Lotus Sutra in the Latter Day of the Law will encounter many persecutions, such as being struck with swords and staves. In other words, this persecution predicted in the Lotus Sutra was inflicted upon Nichiren Daishonin in actuality, which proved that he is the votary of the Lotus Sutra.

As the violence of Hei-no saemon-no-jo and others continued, the Daishonin powerfully remonstrated against them:

> How ridiculous! See how insanely Hei-no saemon-no-jo is
> acting! All of you are now toppling the pillar of Japan.
> (*On the Buddha's Behavior* [Shuju onfurumai-gosho],
> *Gosho*, p. 1058)

Hei-no saemon-no-jo and his retainers, who were on a rampage, were overwhelmed by the Daishonin's unwavering attitude and immediately fell silent. This was Nichiren Daishonin's second remonstration with the nation.

4. The Sado Period

Historical Site of Tsukahara

Tatsunokuchi Persecution—Discarding the Provisional Identity and Revealing the True Identity

On September 12th of the eighth year of Bunnei (1271), Nichiren Daishonin was taken from his hut in Matsubagayatsu and dragged through the streets of Kamakura. He was treated like someone who had committed a serious crime. Then, the Daishonin was taken to the Supreme Court, where he was sentenced to "exile on Sado Island" by Hei-no saemon-no-jo. This "official verdict," however, was nothing but a cover-up. In reality, the government officials' true intention was to behead the Daishonin. In fact, at midnight the Daishonin was taken under guard to the Tatsunokuchi execution grounds.

On their way to the site, the Daishonin dismounted from his horse in front of the Hachiman Shrine at Tsurugaoka (refer to the map on p. 59), and loudly called out to Bodhisattva Hachiman:

Great Bodhisattva Hachiman, are you truly a guardian deity?
(*On the Buddha's Behavior* [Shuju onfurumai-gosho],
Gosho, p. 1059)

He reprimanded Great Bodhisattva Hachiman for not protecting the votary of the Lotus Sutra. Then, after passing Yuigahama Beach, the Daishonin sent a boy named Kumaomaru to inform Shijo Kingo of what was happening. Shijo Kingo immediately rushed to the Daishonin's side and accompanied him to the execution grounds with the resolution to follow his master to the grave. Upon arrival at the site, Shijo Kingo could not control himself and began to sob. The Daishonin chided him, saying:

Why can you not understand! You should be delighted at this great fortune. Have you forgotten what I told you?
(*On the Buddha's Behavior* [Shuju onfurumai-gosho],
Gosho, p. 1060)

At the moment the executioner raised his sword, a luminous orb as bright as a full moon suddenly shot across the sky from the direction of Enoshima Island. The intense light blinded the executioner, causing him to fall down to the ground. The soldiers surrounding the Daishonin were terrified and ran about. Some threw themselves in prostration on the spot. In the end, they were not able to take the Daishonin's life.

This persecution at Tatsunokuchi has an important meaning, in that the Daishonin discarded his provisional identity as the reincarnation of Bodhisattva Jogyo and revealed his true identity as the True Buddha of the infinite past of *kuon-ganjo* with the property of intrinsically perfect wisdom. This is called "discarding the provisional identity and revealing the true identity."

Concerning this matter, the Daishonin states:

> A man by the name of Nichiren was beheaded [as a common mortal] between the hours of the Rat and the Ox[31] on the twelfth day of the ninth month of the previous year. His soul reached Sado Island...
>
> (*The Opening of the Eyes* [Kaimoku-sho], *Gosho*, p. 563)

The word "soul" refers to the soul of the Buddha of the infinite past of *kuon-ganjo* with the property of perfect wisdom. In other words, in the midst of the great persecution at Tatsunokuchi, where the Daishonin had to risk his life, he revealed his life state as the True Buddha of the infinite past of *kuon-ganjo*.

---

31 **The hours of the Rat and Ox**: The hours between 11 p.m. and 3 a.m.

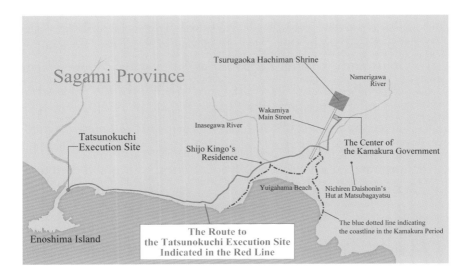

On the Luminous Orb

The Daishonin describes the luminous orb in *Letter to Shijo Kingo* (Shijo kingo dono-goshosoku):

> Among the three guardian deities of light, the guardian deity of the moon appeared in the form of a luminous orb and helped me when I was about to be beheaded at the execution grounds at Tatsunokuchi. The guardian deity of the morning star descended from the heavens to greet me four or five days ago. Now only the guardian deity of the sun remains. He certainly will protect me, which is very reassuring. The Teachers of the Law (*Hosshi*; tenth) chapter of the Lotus Sutra states, "[The Buddha] will dispatch [Buddhas, Bodhisattvas, and guardian deities] in human form to those who propagate

the Lotus Sutra in order to protect them." You should have no doubt about this. Also, the Peaceful Practices (*Anrakugyo*; fourteenth) chapter of the Lotus Sutra states, "Nobody can attack them (the votaries of the Lotus Sutra) with swords and staves." Furthermore, the Universal Gate of Bodhisattva who Perceives the World's Sounds (*Kanzeon bosatsu fumon*; twenty-fifth) chapter of the Lotus Sutra states, "The sword will be instantaneously broken to pieces." These passages in the Lotus Sutra never can be false.

(*Gosho*, p. 479)

As mentioned above, the votaries of the Lotus Sutra will undergo various persecutions, yet they will certainly receive protection from the guardian deities. In particular, the luminous orb, which appeared at Tatsunokuchi, was the materialization of protection from the guardian deity of the moon—one of the three guardian deities of light.

Scientists today, using modern analytical methods, have come up with various explanations of what this luminous ball-like object might have been. Some say that it was lightning or a shooting star. Others say it was a meteor that burned in the atmosphere and exploded into a fireball. No matter what kind of scientific theories are laid out, however, they are nothing but speculation.

The important question is why it appeared at that place, on that night, and at that very moment. In other words, it is a fact that even the government, which wielded absolute power, failed to behead the Daishonin. It is extremely significant that this phenomenon occurred right before the execution attempt and immediately after the Daishonin scolded the guardian deities. There is no explanation other than the truth of this Buddhism for such a mystic concordance of "time." Buddhism elucidates the True Buddha's enlightened power that permeates throughout the entire universe and the profound significance of the principle of the oneness of life and its environment.

In his *Annotations on the Great Concentration and Insight* (Maka shikan guketsu), the Great Teacher Miaole[32] states:

> Therefore, when one attains enlightenment, in accordance with this doctrine (the doctrine of *ichinen sanzen*), one can realize that the physical and spiritual aspects of one's life permeate throughout the entire universe.
>
> (*Guketsu ehon*, vol. 2, p. 296)

He interprets the mystic influence and the life state of the True Buddha, who realized his life is one with the entire universe, based on the principle of the oneness of life and its environment.

This phenomenon of the luminous orb clearly demonstrates that the Daishonin proved the validity of the passage cited above by undergoing the persecution himself. At the same time, he demonstrated his enlightened power as the True Buddha for all living beings.

---

32 The Great Teacher Miaole [711-782]: The sixth patriarch of the Tiantai sect in China, respectfully called the restorer of the Tiantai sect. He wrote *Annotations on the Profound Meaning of the Lotus Sutra* (Hokke gengi shakusen), *Annotations on the Words and Phrases of the Lotus Sutra* (Hokke mongu ki), and *Annotations on the Great Concentration and Insight* (Maka shikan guketsu), in order to advocate the doctrines of the Great Teacher Tiantai.

Sado Exile

After the Tatsunokuchi Persecution, Nichiren Daishonin was held in detention at the Homma residence located at Echi, Sagami Province (presently Atsugi City, Kanagawa Prefecture) for nearly a month. On October tenth of the eighth year of Bunnei (1271), he began his journey from Echi to the place of his exile on Sado. On the 21st day of the same month, he arrived at Teradomari in Echigo (presently Niigata Prefecture). He reached Sado Island on the 28th, and started to live in a hut called Sammaido at Tsukahara (also referred to as Tsukahara Sammaido) on November first.

The Daishonin described his extremely harsh life in the severe cold at the Tsukahara Sammaido as follows:

> (I was taken to a small hut) that was in the middle of a wasteland called Tsukahara in Sado. Only two meters square, it stood on some land where corpses were abandoned, a place like a graveyard on the outskirts of the capital (Kyoto). No statue of the Buddha was enshrined there and the roof and walls were full of holes. The snow fell and piled up, never melting away. I spent night and day there on a fur mat, wearing a straw cape. At night, it constantly hailed and snowed with thunder and lightning. Even in the daytime, the sun hardly shone. It was a wretched place to live.
>
> (*On the Buddha's Behavior* [Shuju onfurumai-gosho], *Gosho*, p. 1062)

Moreover, the islanders of Sado were Nembutsu believers, and the Daishonin's life was always in danger.

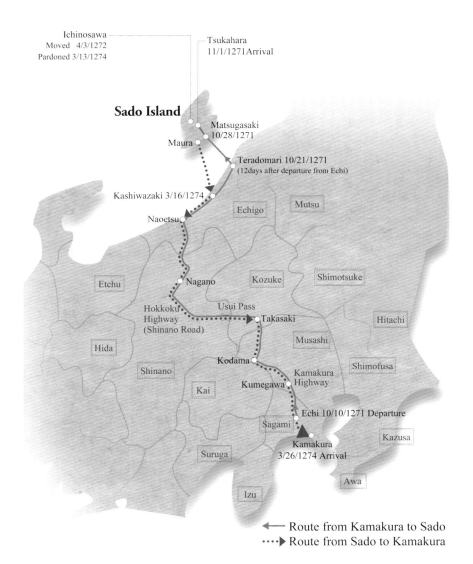

Ichinosawa
Moved 4/3/1272
Pardoned 3/13/1274

Tsukahara
11/1/1271 Arrival

Sado Island

Matsugasaki
10/28/1271

Maura

Teradomari 10/21/1271
(12days after departure from Echi)

Kashiwazaki 3/16/1274

Echigo

Mutsu

Naoetsu

Kozuke

Shimotsuke

Etchu

Nagano

Usui Pass

Hokkoku
Highway
(Shinano Road)

Takasaki

Hitachi

Hida

Musashi

Kodama

Shimofusa

Kamakura
Highway

Shinano

Kumegawa

Kai

Echi 10/10/1271 Departure

Sagami

Kazusa

Suruga

Kamakura
3/26/1274 Arrival

Awa

Izu

⟵ Route from Kamakura to Sado
••••▶ Route from Sado to Kamakura

Tsukahara Debate

On January 16th of the following year, the Daishonin held a debate at Tsukahara with several hundred monks and believers of various sects, in the presence of Homma Rokuro zaemon.[33]

Priests from various sects gathered, one after another, at the Tsukahara Sammaido. They loudly and abusively denounced the Daishonin; it is said that the clamor was like an earthquake or thunder. The Daishonin observed the crowd for a while, and addressed them in a powerful, clear voice:

---

33 Homma Rokuro zaemon [Dates of birth and death unknown]: A magistrate on Sado Island. He kept Nichiren Daishonin under close surveillance during the Daishonin's exile to Sado Island.

Be quiet, all of you. Since you have just traveled all the way [to Tsukahara] in order to defeat me based on your respective doctrines, speaking ill of and cursing me now is futile.

(On the Buddha's Behavior [Shuju onfurumai-gosho],
Gosho, p. 1064)

This was the start of the debate. He described the debate in the Gosho, *On the Buddha's Behavior* (Shuju onfurumai-gosho):

The priests referred to the doctrines of the *Great Concentration and Insight* (Maka shikan), Shingon, and Nembutsu. For each statement they made, I carefully clarified the meaning of what they said and let them concur. Then, in return, I challenged them by strictly questioning them, and pressed them for answers. However, they could only say a few words, and then they fell silent. They were inferior to the Shingon, Zen, Nembutsu, and Tendai priests in Kamakura. You could imagine how the debate went. It was like cutting a gourd with a sharp sword, or a heavy wind bending the grass.

(Gosho, pp. 1064-1065)

Even learned priests of the major temples in Kamakura could not defeat the Daishonin in a debate. How could the priests on Sado or those from northern Japan defy him? In the same Gosho, the Daishonin goes on to describe the behavior of these priests:

[The Nembutsu believers and the Shingon, Zen, and Tendai priests] not only had a poor understanding of the Buddhist doctrines, but also contradicted themselves. They forgot the distinction between sutras and treatises, and between annotations and treatises...some became silent, others turned pale, while others declared that the teaching of Nembutsu was wrong. Some of them even spontaneously discarded their surplice and flat-shaped prayer beads (of the Nembutsu sect), and made a pledge in writing that they would never chant the Nembutsu again.

(*Gosho*, p. 1065)

Thus, the debate ended in an instant, due to the Daishonin's true reasoning.

As Homma Rokuro zaemon was leaving after the debate, the Daishonin made a prediction that an uprising would occur in Kamakura in the near future.

A month later, the Daishonin's prediction came true. An internal conflict occurred within the Hojo clan, which is known as the February Incident. Since the Daishonin's prediction proved to be true, some of the islanders on Sado began to hold him in awe.

Disturbance among Nichiren Daishonin's Followers

After the Tatsunokuchi Persecution, Nichiren Daishonin's disciples and lay believers were also severely persecuted and suffered from tremendous hardships. The Daishonin states in *Reply to Shijo Kingo* (Shijo kingo dono-gohenji):

> Several years ago, when I, Nichiren, incurred the Shogunate's wrath, all the people throughout Japan hated me. Many of my disciples had their manors confiscated by their lords, and some believers in various places were disowned by their lords, while others were evicted from their lord's properties.
>
> (*Gosho*, p. 1117)

He also mentions in *On Persecutions Befalling the Buddha* (Shonin gonan ji):

> Innumerable disciples of mine were killed, injured, expelled, or had fines levied against them.
>
> (*Gosho*, p. 1396)

Among the Daishonin's lay believers, some of them had their properties confiscated, some were driven out by their lords and lost their means to make a living, and others were expelled from the land controlled by their lords.

The Daishonin states in *Reply to Nii ama* (Nii ama gozen-gohenji):

> Also in Kamakura, when the government accused me, 999 out of 1,000 believers discarded their faith.
>
> (*Gosho*, p. 765)

Some of the Daishonin's followers not only discarded their faith in his teachings, but also arrogantly criticized and slandered him. He states in *Letter from Sado* (Sado-gosho):

> When people, who appeared to believe in Nichiren, see persecutions befalling me, they harbor doubts and abandon the Lotus Sutra. These people with such distorted views would even instruct Nichiren and regard themselves wiser than me. This is truly pathetic, because they will lapse into *avichi* hell (hell of incessant suffering) much longer than even the Nembutsu believers....These people say that although Nichiren is their master, he is too aggressive, and they will propagate the Lotus Sutra in a more amiable way. This is just like fireflies, with their faint glow, laughing at the bright sun and moon, a lowly anthill looking down upon the towering Mount Hua, a small inlet despising vast rivers and seas, or magpies ridiculing a phoenix.
>
> (*Gosho*, p. 583)

Among those who discarded their faith, some were well known. The Daishonin mentioned this in *Reply to Ueno* (Ueno dono-gohenji):

> My former disciples like Sho-bo, Noto-bo, and Nagoe-no ama were greedy, cowardly, and ignorant, but they called themselves wise. Because of this, when the great persecutions happened [to Nichiren], those individuals caused many people to quit their practice.
>
> (*Gosho*, p. 1123)

As stated above, many of Nichiren Daishonin's disciples and lay believers abandoned their practice as well as their master. Still, some of them maintained strong faith in the Daishonin's true Buddhism.

Nichiren Daishonin Encourages his Followers

Nichiren Daishonin was concerned that many of his believers in Shimofusa Province might be discouraged in their faith, and therefore, on October fifth, he sent the Gosho titled *The Doctrine of Lessening one's Karmic Retribution* (Tenju kyoju homon) to three of his followers, Ota, Soya, and Kimbara.[34] In this Gosho, he explains the significance of overcoming the persecutions, which will come from the propagation of the true Law. A passage in this Gosho reads:

> If one's heavy negative karma accumulated since one's past existences is not eradicated in this lifetime, then he is destined to undergo the sufferings of hell in the future. However, if he encounters severe persecutions in this lifetime, the sufferings of hell will instantly disappear, and after his death, he will receive the benefit of reaching the states of humanity, rapture, the three vehicles, or the one vehicle of Buddhahood.
>
> (*Gosho*, p. 480)

In this passage, the Daishonin taught the significance of lessening one's karmic retribution to his followers by saying that this was the

---

34 **Kimbara [Dates of birth and death unknown]:** One of the followers of Nichiren Daishonin. He received the Gosho, *The Doctrine of Lessening one's Karmic Retribution* (Tenju kyoju homon), with Ota saemon-no-jo and Soya nyudo.

time for them to do so.

Immediately before his departure to Sado, the Daishonin sent a Gosho to Gijo-bo and Joken-bo of Seichoji Temple, as well as his followers in that area. This writing, titled *Incurring the Displeasure of the Authorities Leading to the Sado Exile* (Sado gokanki-sho) was dated October tenth. A passage in this Gosho reads:

> As for the path to becoming a Buddha, it can be concluded that one can attain Buddhahood only by enduring an event that might put one's life at risk....Only by going through such hardships could I read the Lotus Sutra with my life. With this understanding, I can summon up even more faith and look forward to my next life....If I can lay down my life, a life that would have been lost in vain, for the sake of the Lotus Sutra, it will be likened to turning a stone into gold. Thus, each one of you need not lament over my circumstances.
>
> (*Gosho*, pp. 482-483)

The Daishonin shows the path to attaining enlightenment through his behavior of enduring a great persecution that might take his life for the sake of the Lotus Sutra. He discarded his provisional identity and revealed his true identity by undergoing the persecution at Tatsunokuchi, and now is about to be banished. He describes his joy of having proven the validity of the Lotus Sutra through these actions. Even in the face of great persecutions, the Daishonin always thought about and encouraged his followers to develop unwavering faith.

Relocation to Ichinosawa

> Around the summer of the ninth year of Bunnei (1272),
> when I was living in a place called Ichinosawa, located in
> Ishida Village in Sado Province…
>
> (*Letter to the Wife of Ichinosawa nyudo*
> [Ichinosawa nyudo nyobo-gosho], *Gosho*, p. 829)

We can assume from the above Gosho passage that the Daishonin had been taken from Tsukahara to Ichinosawa in Ishida Village by early summer of 1272.

The reason for the relocation is not clear. One possible reason is that the government developed a feeling of awe towards the Daishonin, because his prediction of internal strife within the government came true with the occurrence of the February Incident.

About his life in Ichinosawa, the Daishonin states in the *Letter to the Wife of Ichinosawa nyudo* (Ichinosawa nyudo nyobo-gosho):

> (Even) farmers delegated by the government office to
> distribute food and other items, seemed to harbor intense
> hatred toward me, both publicly and personally. They hated
> me more than even a foe of their parents or a longtime enemy.
>
> (*Gosho*, p. 829)

Homma Yamashiro nyudo,[35] who was appointed by Homma Shigetsura to keep an eye on the Daishonin, was a strong Nembutsu believer; therefore, he treated the Daishonin harshly. Although

---

35 **Homma Yamashiro nyudo [Dates of birth and death unknown]:** His official name is Homma Yasunobu. During Nichiren Daishonin's banishment to Sado Island, Yamashiro nyudo kept Nichiren Daishonin under close surveillance after the Daishonin was moved to Ichinosawa.

Ichinosawa nyudo, the owner of the residence, to which the Daishonin was transferred, was also a Nembutsu believer, he gradually developed a sense of respect for the Daishonin as he observed the Daishonin's behavior.

In the *Letter to the Wife of Ichinosawa nyudo* (Ichinosawa nyudo nyobo-gosho) the Daishonin wrote:

> The steward (Ichinosawa nyudo) of my place of exile had compassion for me deep in his heart. Although on the surface he appeared to be rigid towards me, he seemed to feel truly sorry for me. No matter how much time goes by, I will never forget this.
>
> (*Gosho*, p. 829)

Compared to the Tsukahara Sammaido, which was nothing more than an abandoned hut, the dwelling place in Ichinosawa was considerably better. However, by this time, there were more disciples who accompanied the Daishonin, and they were suffering from lack of food.

He described his life in the *Letter to the Wife of Ichinosawa nyudo* (Ichinosawa nyudo nyobo-gosho):

> The food given by the farmers was not sufficient. Because many disciples accompanied me, we barely had a few mouthfuls of rice, placed on wooden trays [without proper dishes] or directly into our hands.
>
> (*Gosho*, p. 829)

Sado Island

O-Sado Mountains

▲
Mount Kimboku

Ichinosawa ●
Nakaoki ○

Kuninaka
Plain

The Site of the Governor's Residence ○ ● **Tsukahara**

Ko-Sado Mountains

Ogura
Pass

Matsugasaki ○

Maura ○

Ichinosawa, Sado Island

Restraining the Disciples' Efforts to Obtain a Pardon

At that time in Kamakura, some of the Daishonin's disciples were petitioning the authorities to issue Nichiren Daishonin a pardon. However, the Daishonin strictly instructed them through Toki Jonin to restrain their activities. This is because the Daishonin did not need to yield to the government by asking for a pardon, as if he were to blame. Rather, his true intention was to open the blind eyes of influential government officials who were ruling Japan and save all the people in the country. Therefore, in May of the ninth year of Bunnei (1272), the Daishonin severely warned his disciples in *The Distinction between the Lotus Sutra and Erroneous Teachings such as the Shingon Sect* (Shingon shoshu imoku):

> If any of my disciples behaves in a manner that might indicate Nichiren is begging the authorities to pardon him from exile, such a disciple is unfaithful (to Nichiren). Under no circumstances would I ever save such a person in his next life, either. Each one of you must understand this matter.
>
> (*Gosho*, p. 602)

Toki Jonin was grieving over the fact that Nichiren Daishonin had not been pardoned. So the Daishonin sent him the Gosho, *Reply to Toki* (Toki dono-gohenji) in July of the tenth year of Bunnei (1273). He encouraged Toki and all the other followers by expressing his conviction that the true Law would prevail. He stated:

> You should not lament over the fact that I have not been pardoned from exile. I am fully aware of the cause of misfortunes in Japan. Some of the predictions in my letter

of remonstration have already occurred, and others are yet to occur. Regardless of whether Nichiren survives or not, the five characters of Myoho-Renge-Kyo will prevail without doubt.

(*Gosho*, p. 679)

Nichiren Daishonin's life in Ichinosawa was not easy. However, through daily interactions with the Daishonin, Ichinosawa nyudo and his family members gradually understood the significance of faith in the true teaching and in the end, they came to protect the Daishonin. Moreover, the Daishonin's disciples and lay believers who resided far and near started to send him various offerings.

The Pardon from Sado Exile

In the 11th year of Bunnei (1274), an emissary from the Mongolian empire again came to Japan. Thus, Nichiren Daishonin's prediction of the disaster of invasion from foreign lands seemed to be coming true. Moreover, natural disasters occurring one after another caused even further confusion throughout the nation. The people of Japan were spending their days in constant anxiety. Seeing these chaotic phenomena and concluding that Nichiren Daishonin was exiled for no reason, Hojo Tokimune, the regent of the Kamakura government at the time, issued a pardon for the Daishonin on February 14th of the same year.

The letter of pardon was delivered to the Daishonin on March eighth, and he and his followers left Ichinosawa on Sado Island on the 13th day of the same month. On the way to Kamakura, Nembutsu believers in Echigo (current Niigata Prefecture) and Shinano (current Nagano Prefecture) Provinces gathered at Zenkoji

Temple, planning to ambush and kill the Daishonin. However, they were not able to carry out an attack, since the Daishonin was escorted by soldiers. Nichiren Daishonin arrived safely in Kamakura on the 26th day of the same month.

During the Daishonin's two-and-a-half-year exile on Sado Island, Nikko Shonin devotedly served him. During that time, Abutsu-bo[36] and his wife Sennichi ama,[37] Ko nyudo and his wife Ko ama,[38] Sairen-bo,[39] Nakaoki nyudo,[40] and other people living on Sado became the Daishonin's followers.

---

36 Abutsu-bo [1189-1279]: His full name is Abutsu-bo Nittoku. He became a follower of Nichiren Daishonin while the Daishonin was living in exile on Sado Island. He was one of the main Hokkeko believers of Sado. His wife was Sennichi ama. Despite his advanced age of 90, he made a pilgrimage multiple times to visit the Daishonin in Mount Minobu.

37 Sennichi ama [?-1302]: She became Nichiren Daishonin's believer with her husband, Abutsu-bo, and devotedly protected the Daishonin, when he was exiled to Sado Island. She supported Abutsu-bo so that he could make pilgrimages to Mount Minobu, where the Daishonin resided.

38 Ko nyudo and Ko ama [Dates of birth and death unknown]: A couple who were Nichiren Dasihonin's followers on Sado Island. They were on friendly terms with Abutsu-bo and his wife. During the banishment of Nichiren Daishonin to Sado Island, they devotedly protected the Daishonin. Ko ama supported Ko nyudo when he visited the Daishonin twice at Mount Minobu. They were given the Goshos, including *Reply to Ko nyudo* (Ko nyudo dono-gohenji).

39 Sairen-bo [?-1308]: A priest who originally studied the Tendai doctrine. He became Nichiren Daishonin's disciple during his exile to Sado Island.

40 Nakaoki nyudo [Dates of birth and death unknown]: One of Nichiren Daishonin's followers on Sado Island. He lived in Nakaoki on Sado Island. It is said that he, his father, and his entire family practiced Nichiren Daishonin's Buddhism. He was given the Gosho, *Letter to Nakaoki nyudo* (Nakaoki nyudo-goshosoku) by the Daishonin.

Gosho Writings on Sado Island

During his exile on Sado, the Daishonin authored more than 50 writings, including *On the Heritage of the Ultimate Law of Life and Death* (Shoji ichidaiji kechimyaku-sho), *The True Entity of All Phenomena* (Shoho jisso-sho), and *On the Meaning of the True Entity of Myoho-Renge-Kyo* (Totaigi-sho). The most significant Goshos among these writings are *The Opening of the Eyes* (Kaimoku-sho) and *The True Object of Worship* (Kanjin no honzon-sho). In February of the ninth year of Bunnei (1272), the Daishonin wrote *The Opening of the Eyes* in the severe cold at the Tsukahara Sammaido, where paper and *sumi* ink were scarce.

There were basically two major reasons why this Gosho was written. One was to open up the blind eyes of all living beings, who are ignorant of the teachings of true Buddhism, and to lead all the people in the Latter Day of the Law to the Daishonin's true teaching. The other reason was to encourage the Daishonin's disciples and lay believers, who were deeply discouraged due to the Daishonin's exile. Many of them were on the verge of abandoning their faith, while others already had forsaken their faith.

In this Gosho, the Daishonin reveals that he, himself, is the votary of the Lotus Sutra, as he had undergone persecutions that had put his life at risk. He also clearly states that he is the Buddha to be revered by all people in the Latter Day of the Law who possesses the three virtues of sovereign, teacher, and parent. For these reasons, this Gosho is said to be the treatise that revealed the object of worship in terms of the person.

The Daishonin wrote *The True Object of Worship* at Ichinosawa on Sado Island on April 25th in the following year. The Daishonin states:

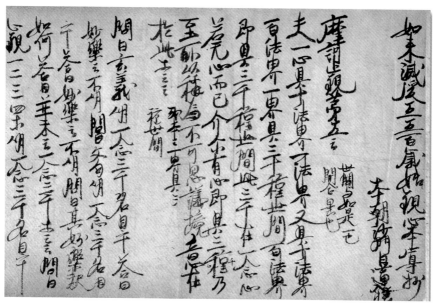

Above: *The True Object of Worship*
(handwritten by Nichiren Daishonin, stored at Nakayama Hokekyoji Temple
of Nichiren-shu sect)

Right: *The Opening of the Eyes*
(a handwritten copy)

[What is described in *The True Object of Worship* is] the most significant to Nichiren.

(*Cover Letter to the True Object of Worship* [Kanjin no honzon-sho soejo], *Gosho*, p. 662)

This Gosho reveals that the Daishonin makes his advent as the True Buddha at the beginning of the Latter Day of the Law and establishes the Gohonzon of the sowing hidden in the depths of the Life Span chapter of the Lotus Sutra for all living beings. For this reason, this Gosho is said to be the treatise that reveals the object of worship in terms of the Law.

The Daishonin states:

You should realize that the doctrines [expounded by Nichiren] prior to my exile to Sado Province correspond to Shakyamuni's pre-Lotus Sutra teachings.

(*Letter to Misawa* [Misawa-sho], *Gosho*, p. 1204)

This means that there is a profound difference between the Daishonin's doctrines and behavior before and after he discarded his provisional identity and revealed his true identity. In other words, prior to the Sado Exile, the Daishonin propagated his teachings as the reincarnation of Bodhisattva Jogyo (Superior Practice). Therefore, he did not inscribe the Gohonzon before Sado. However, after he discarded his provisional identity and revealed his true identity, he began to inscribe the Gohonzon and lead all living beings as the True Buddha of the Latter Day of the Law.

5. The Minobu Period

Minobu

The Third Remonstration with the Nation

On April eighth in the 11th year of Bunnei (1274), Nichiren Daishonin met with Hei-no saemon-no-jo Yoritsuna and several other Kamakura government officials.

Although Hei-no saemon-no-jo had taken a threatening attitude toward Nichiren Daishonin during the Tatsunokuchi affairs, this time, he welcomed the Daishonin with a gentle demeanor. He asked some questions, including the possibility of attaining Buddhahood through the pre-Lotus Sutra teachings, and the timing of the Mongol attack.

Nichiren Daishonin replied that the Buddhist sects based on the pre-Lotus Sutra teachings could not lead their followers to attain Buddhahood. He also admonished them, stating that, if the Kamakura government continued its policy of ordering the priests of the Shingon sect to offer prayers for protection from the Mongol invasion, Japan would fall into decay without fail. The Daishonin further warned that since the guardian deities obviously were angry, it was certain that the Mongol attack would occur within the year. The Daishonin therefore admonished Hei-no saemon-no-jo to immediately discard all erroneous doctrines and embrace the Daishonin's true Buddhism.

Among the Daishonin's warnings, the government officials were only afraid that his prediction of a foreign invasion actually would come true. They made an offer to establish a temple for the Daishonin in Kamakura. But they also asked him to agree to offer prayers for the peace and security of the nation together with the priests of other sects. The Daishonin completely rejected their proposal.

The Daishonin had no desire for fame or the power of government patronage. Rather, his aspiration was only to lead the people to take faith in the true Law and realize a peaceful land by vanquishing the cause of misfortune, that is, heretical teachings.

Kaga-no-hoin's Prayer for Rain

Having seen the hopeless situation in which the wells had dried up and the crops had withered due to frequent droughts, the Kamakura government decided to take measures by ordering Kaga-no-hoin, the chief priest of the Amidado Hall in Kamakura, to conduct a ritual prayer for rain, despite the Daishonin's third remonstration that the government should never order or request prayers to be made by the Shingon sect.

This priest was a high-ranking monk, enjoying the greatest prestige at that time. As the principal scholar of Toji Temple, the central temple of the Shingon sect in Kyoto at that time, he was said to have mastered the secret arts of the Shingon sect and to have thoroughly learned various other teachings, such as Kegon and

Tendai.

On April tenth of the 11th year of Bunnei (1274), Kaga-no-hoin started to pray for rain. On the following day, it started to rain. All day long, there was no wind blowing and the rain quietly continued.

Hojo Tokimune, the regent of the Kamakura government, was so impressed that he gave the monk a variety of rewards, such as gold and horses.

Thus, all the people in Kamakura mocked the Daishonin, and said, "Although Nichiren was about to be beheaded due to the propagation of his incorrect teachings, he luckily survived. Despite that, he continues to slander the Nembutsu and Zen sects rather than conduct himself properly. He is even slandering the Shingon sect. This time, the prayer for rain came true with the Shingon esoteric teaching. This serves as a good example of its power. Nichiren's doctrines were defeated, and the Shingon sect won a victory."

Even some of the Daishonin's disciples began to harbor doubts. They wondered, "Our master insists that prayers for rain based on the teachings of Shingon never will be answered, but his teaching might be wrong." Upon hearing this, the Daishonin explained to them as follows:

If the evil doctrines of Kobo,[41] who is revered as a great teacher in the Shingon sect, were true and prayers based on his teachings were beneficial for the nation, then Emperor Gotoba, who was exiled to Oki Island, should have been victorious during the Jokyu Incident. Kobo wrote in the *Treatise of the Ten Stages of the Mind* (Ju jushin-ron) that the

---

41 Kobo [774-835]: Also known as Kukai or the Great Teacher Kobo, who founded the Shingon sect in Japan. The Daishonin refuted this sect, saying, "Shingon will ruin the nation."

Lotus Sutra is inferior even to the Flower Garland Sutra. Moreover, in *The Precious Key to the Secret Treasury* (Hizo hoyaku) he stated that Shakyamuni Buddha, who is described in the *Juryo* chapter of the Lotus Sutra, is nothing but a common mortal. He called the Great Teacher Tiantai[42] a thief, and furthermore claimed that the Buddha who preached the Lotus Sutra, the teaching of the one vehicle of Buddhahood, was inferior even to the sandal-bearer of Great Sun Tathagata.[43] Kaga-no-hoin is a disciple of Kobo, who taught these heretical doctrines. How could he possibly defeat me in a challenge to pray for rain? If he could do that, then the Dragon King, who brings forth the rain, would become an enemy of the Lotus Sutra. He would be strictly punished by the Heavenly Kings Daibon and Taishaku[44] and the Four Heavenly Kings.[45] Thus, there must be a deep reason for this appearance of rain.

(*Gosho*, pp. 1068-1069 [Summary])

On April 12th, soon after the Daishonin gave this explanation, it stopped raining, and violent winds suddenly began to blow. Both

---

42 The Great Teacher Tiantai [538-597]: A Chinese priest during the Chen and Sui dynasties, who was the founder of the Tiantai sect in China and established its doctrines based on the Lotus Sutra. His lectures were recorded in the three major writings of the Tiantai sect: *Profound Meaning of the Lotus Sutra* (Hokke gengi), *Words and Phrases of the Lotus Sutra* (Hokke mongu), and *Great Concentration and Insight* (Maka shikan).

43 The Great Sun Tathagata: The Buddha who appears in the Great Sun Tathagata Sutra *(Dainichi-kyo)* and other sutras. He is considered to be the most important Buddha in the esoteric Shingon teachings.

44 The Heavenly Kings Daibon and Taishaku: The guardian deities who vowed to protect Buddhism as well as the votaries of the Lotus Sutra in the Latter Day of the Law.

45 The Four Heavenly Kings: The Heavenly King of the East (Jpn. *Jikokuten*, Skt. *Dhrtarashtra*), the Heavenly King of the West (Jpn. *Komokuten*, Skt. *Virupaksha*), the Heavenly King of the North (Jpn. *Bishamonten*, Skt. *Vaishravana*), and the Heavenly King of the South (Jpn. *Zochoten*, Skt. *Virudhaka*).

small and large houses, temple halls and pagodas, big trees, the government buildings, and so on, were destroyed by the gale force winds. A huge luminous orb flew through the sky. Many people and animals, such as oxen and horses, were killed by the powerful winds. It was unprecedented for such strong gales to appear at that time of year, which was not the typhoon season in Japan. Moreover, the storms did not blow throughout Japan, but only in the eight provinces of the Kanto region. It is said that the winds blew harder in Sagami Province than in the other seven provinces, and within Sagami Province, they blew most forcefully in Kamakura. And within Kamakura, the winds blew even more intensely at the government buildings, Tsurugaoka Hachiman Shrine, Kenchoji Temple, and Gokurakuji Temple.

Regarding this tragic phenomenon, the *Record of the Nine Reigns under the Hojo* (Hojo kudai ki), a historical document, states:

> On the twelfth day in the fourth month of the eleventh year of Bunnei (1274), violent winds swept [the land] causing the plants and trees to die.
> *(The Collection of the Japanese Classics, the second series* [Zoku gunsho ruiju], vol. 29-1, p. 425*)*

Nichiren Daishonin also refers to this tragedy in *Repaying Debts of Gratitude* (Ho-on-sho):

> The violent wind on the twelfth day of the fourth month in the eleventh year of Bunnei (1274) blew against the prayer for rain offered by Kaga-no-hoin, who is the chief priest of the Amidado Hall, and is called the wisest person of Toji Temple. He must have received the transmission of the evil

Law without any changes from Shan Wu Wei,[46] Vajrabodhi,[47] and Amoghavajra.[48]

(*Gosho*, p. 1024)

This was actual proof of the failure of Kaga-no-hoin's prayer for rain. In fact, his prayers brought about tragic and disastrous results, exposing the fallacy of Shingon prayers. The people of Kamakura and Kaga-no-hoin's disciples who ridiculed the Daishonin were now left dumbfounded after witnessing such a tragic result, and the Daishonin's disciples also were stunned by the fact that his prediction came true.

He stated the following in the Gosho, *On Establishing the Hachiman Shrine* (Hachimangu zoei no koto):

On the twelfth day of the fourth month in the eleventh year of Bunnei (1274), a violent wind blew. This was an omen indicating that the invasion from foreign lands would occur later that same year. The wind is an envoy of the heaven and the earth. This is what is referred to as, "when the politics are rough, the winds get rough."

(*Gosho*, pp. 1557-1558)

The Daishonin declared that this violent storm was an omen of the invasion of Japan by the Mongols.

---

46 Shan Wu Wei [637-735]: A priest from India. His Sanskrit name was Subhakarasimha. He first introduced the esoteric Shingon teachings to China. One of the three Tripitaka masters referred to in the Gosho along with Vajrabodhi and Amoghavajra.

47 Vajrabodhi [669-741]: A priest from India. One of the three Tripitaka masters who established the foundation of the esoteric Shingon teachings in China.

48 Amoghavajra [705-774]: A priest of the esoteric Shingon teachings in China. A disciple of Shan Wu Wei. One of the three Tripitaka masters.

He also stated:

> The Kamakura Shogunate should never order the monks of the Shingon sect to incant a spell for the Mongols to perish. If they do, the nation will fall to ruin even more quickly....Judging by the signs from the heavens, which show the guardian deities becoming increasingly furious, it will not be long before the Mongols arrive and invade the land. The invasion is likely to happen before the end of this year.
>
> (*The Selection of the Time* [Senji-sho], *Gosho*, p. 867)

The Daishonin's prophecy came true as forewarned to Hei-no saemon-no-jo, and in October of the same year (1274) a large Mongolian army attacked Japan. This was an unprecedented incident called the "Battle of Bunnei."

Entering Mount Minobu

Nichiren Daishonin remonstrated with the Kamakura government three times up until then, but his remonstrations were not heard. Therefore, in May of the 11th year of Bunnei (1274), at the age of 53, Nichiren Daishonin went to Mount Minobu to take up residence, following the words of an old proverb,[49] which stated, "If a sage remonstrates with the sovereign three times, and his remonstrations are not heeded, the sage should retire to a mountain."

Minobu was located in Kai Province (currently Yamanashi

---

49 **An old proverb:** Quoted in Goshos, such as *Repaying Debts of Gratitude* (Ho-on-sho). The *Book of Rites* (Rai ki) in ancient China states, "If one remonstrates with the sovereign three times, and his remonstrations are not heeded, he should leave the sovereign."

Prefecture). It was a secluded area, surrounded by towering mountains. The lord of Minobu was Hakiri Sanenaga,[50] who was led to Nichiren Daishonin's Buddhism by Nikko Shonin.

The Daishonin described his journey from Kamakura to Minobu in the *Letter to Toki* (Toki dono-gosho):

> We stayed at Sakawa on the twelfth day [of the fifth month], Takenoshita on the thirteenth day, Kurumagaeshi on the fourteenth day, Omiya on the fifteenth day, and Nambu on the sixteenth day. Then, we finally reached this place (the manor of Hakiri Sanenaga) on the seventeenth day.
>
> (*Gosho*, p. 730)

We can have a better understanding of the Daishonin's journey if we use the current names of the places he passed through. We would say that after departing from Kamakura, he stayed at the following locations:

- May 12th: Sakawa in Odawara City in Kanagawa Prefecture
- May 13th: Takenoshita near the current Ashigara Station in Sunto County in Shizuoka Prefecture
- May 14th: Kurumagaeshi near the Sammaibashi in Numazu City
- May 15th: Omiya (currently Fujinomiya City)
- May 16th: Nambu in Minamikoma County in Yamanashi Prefecture
- May 17th: The residence of Hakiri Sanenaga in Hakiri Village

---

50 Hakiri Sanenaga [1223-1297]: Also called Nambu Rokuro Saburo. Since his inherited estate was called Nambu, he took it for his family name. Nikko Shonin led him to embrace Nichiren Daishonin's Buddhism. He donated the land for Minobu-san Kuonji Temple to Nichiren Daishonin. After the Daishonin's passing, he committed many slanderous acts against the Law, causing Nikko Shonin to leave Mount Minobu.

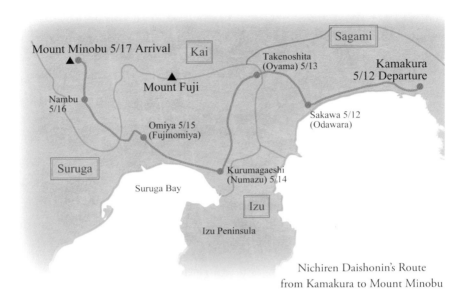

Nichiren Daishonin's Route
from Kamakura to Mount Minobu

Along the way, the Daishonin was eager to see Takahashi nyudo,[51] one of Nikko Shonin's relatives, who lived in Kashima in Fuji County (currently Fuji City). He was a faithful believer and also a key person among the lay believers in the region. The Daishonin trusted him deeply and was looking forward to meeting him again.

However, the region was under the jurisdiction of the main lineage of the Hojo clan. The mother of Hojo Tokimune was a dedicated follower of Ryokan of Gokurakuji Temple, and she had great influence in the region. The Daishonin was concerned that his stay would bring trouble to the Takahashi family, so he decided

---

51 **Takahashi nyudo [Dates of birth and death unknown]:** Takahasi Rokuro Hyoe nyudo. One of the followers during Nichiren Daishonin's lifetime. He was one of the immediate vassals of the Kamakura Shogunate, who lived in Kashima in Fuji County of Suruga Province (currently Motoichiba in Fuji City, Shizuoka Prefecture). It is said that he took faith in Nichiren Daishonin's Buddhism through shakubuku by Nikko Shonin who was his relative. He was given the Goshos, such as *Reply to Takahashi nyudo* (Takahashi nyudo dono-gohenji).

against paying a visit to Takahashi nyudo. Later, the Daishonin wrote to him and explained his decision:

> A thousand times, I was overwhelmed with the urge to meet you again, but I managed to hold myself back and passed by your residence.
> (*Reply to Takahashi nyudo* [Takahashi nyudo dono-gohenji], *Gosho*, p. 889)

Thus, the Daishonin and his disciples arrived at Minobu. However, regarding his stay in Minobu, the Daishonin wrote in *Letter to Toki* (Toki dono-gosho), stating:

> Although I have not yet decided [whether I should settle down here or not], the circumstances in this mountain mostly satisfy my requirements. Therefore, I will stay here for now.
> (*Gosho*, p. 730)

Also, in another Gosho, *Letter to Shimoyama* (Shimoyama-goshosoku), he stated:

> I entered this mountain to stay for the time being.
> (*Gosho*, p. 1153)

We can see from these passages that the Daishonin had no intention to stay in Minobu permanently. The Daishonin only agreed to follow Nikko Shonin's suggestion to go to Minobu. Although in later ages the other Nichiren sects insist that Minobu is the center of the Daishonin's Buddhism, it is obvious from these passages that this interpretation does not reflect the Daishonin's true intention.

Life in Minobu

Nichiren Daishonin wrote the following about the situation when he began to live in Minobu in the postscript to the *Letter to Toki* (Toki dono-gosho), which was written in the 11th year of Bunnei (1274):

> Our hunger is beyond description. Even a cup of rice is not available here. We certainly will starve to death. I have let my disciples [who accompanied me to Minobu] return [to their home regions], and I will remain here all by myself.
>
> (*Gosho*, p.730)

Due to famine throughout Japan, farmers did not have even a cup of rice to sell to anyone. Therefore, the Daishonin and his disciples had to even worry about starving to death. We can understand the gravity of the hardships the Daishonin was facing in Minobu by the fact that he had to let most of his disciples return to their respective home regions.

Moreover, they had to endure the cold of severe winters. Even though lay believers from around the country sent offerings of food and other necessities to the Daishonin, it was not quite enough to support him and a number of his disciples, so they were forced to live frugally in Minobu.

Nichiren Daishonin described the conditions of his life in Mount Minobu as follows:

I kept myself alive by eating snow as Su Wu[52] did, and I survived

---

52 **Su Wu [140 BCE-60 BCE]:** One of the vassals of the Former Han dynasty in ancient China. He was caught by and became a prisoner of the Xiongnu, but he did not give in

[in a mountain] by wearing a straw cape as Li Ling [53] did. When I could not collect anything in the forest, I subsisted without eating anything for three days. When my deerskin [coat] tore, I had no adequate clothing for three or four months.

(*On Offering of an Unlined Cloth* [Tanne-sho], *Gosho*, p. 904)

Here on Mount Minobu, there are many stones, but no rice cakes. Moss is plentiful, but there is nothing to use as a floor covering.

(*Offering of Three Straw Mats* [Mushiro sammai-gosho], *Gosho*, p. 1592)

to their oppression and remained loyal to his sovereign. His story is referenced in several Goshos.

53 Li Ling [?-74 BCE]: One of the generals of the Former Han dynasty in ancient China. He defeated an army of the Xiongnu with a small number of soldiers, but ultimately surrendered to them. Later on, he died in the territory of the Xiongnu. His story is referenced in Goshos such as *Letter to Ko ama* (Ko ama gozen-gosho).

Two years after entering Minobu, in the second year of Kenji (1276), he wrote the following in *On Leaving the Sutra Book Behind* (Bojikyo ji):

> The sound of the recitation of the Lotus Sutra reverberates through the blue sky, and the words of the lectures on the one vehicle echo in the mountains.
>
> (*Gosho*, p. 957)

We can see that the Daishonin spent his daily life in Minobu reciting the Lotus Sutra together with his disciples and lay believers, giving them lectures.

Furthermore, according to the Gosho, *Reply to Hyoe-sakan* (Hyoe sakan dono-gohenji), by the first year of Koan (1278), there were at least 40 to a maximum of 60 people staying in the vicinity of the Daishonin's hut, seeking his guidance and devoting themselves to the practice and study of his Buddhism. In this manner, the Daishonin's hut turned into a lively place with more and more of his disciples and believers visiting him.

This is described in *Reply to Soya* (Soya dono-gohenji), written in August of the second year of Koan (1279), which states:

> This year, I support more than 100 disciples and believers in this mountain. I have them read the Lotus Sutra, and I expound to them on the teaching of the sutra all day long.
>
> (*Gosho*, p. 1386)

Many people who had any relationship with the Daishonin's disciples or believers revered him and came to see him. The number of visitors sometimes swelled to more than 100. Furthermore, some people, including a Nembutsu priest in Shimoyama named Nichiei, tried to listen to his preaching secretly, as written in *Letter to Shimoyama* (Shimoyama-goshosoku):

> Someone sneaked into my dwelling and eavesdropped my lecture behind others....

(Gosho, p. 1137)

Under these circumstances, the Daishonin wrote doctrinal documents and other writings in Mount Minobu. *The Essentials of the Lotus Sutra* (Hokke shuyo-sho) was especially significant. In this Gosho, he revealed for the first time, the name and composition of the Three Great Secret Laws: the True Object of Worship of the Essential Teaching, the High Sanctuary of the Essential Teaching, and the Daimoku of the Essential Teaching.

In November of the second year of Kenji (1276) Nichimoku Shonin, who later became the Third High Priest, visited Nichiren

Daishonin at the age of 17 and began to constantly serve the Daishonin. He had become a disciple of Nikko Shonin in Enzobo Temple in Izu Province in April of the same year.

While chanting Daimoku and reciting the Lotus Sutra, in order to repay the four debts of gratitude,[54] Nichiren Daishonin, in Minobu, educated his disciples and laid the foundation for the perpetuation of the Law and the achievement of kosen-rufu.

Orally Transmitted Teachings (Ongi kuden) and *Recorded Lectures* (Onko kikigaki)

Nichiren Daishonin preached to the priests and lay believers on the true meaning of the Lotus Sutra, which he had revealed at the risk of his life through undergoing the persecutions as predicted in the sutra. His lectures included not only interpretations of the words and phrases of the Lotus Sutra, but also the profound doctrine from the standpoint of the True Buddha in the Latter Day of the Law. Each word and phrase that the Daishonin expounded jolted their spirits, as they etched the teachings firmly and deeply into their hearts.

However, it was not easy for everyone to understand the profound significance of the Daishonin's lectures, which reveal the Buddhism of the sowing hidden in the depths of the Lotus Sutra.

Nikko Shonin was the only one who was able to comprehend the deep meaning of the Daishonin's teachings, since he completely and perfectly understood the Daishonin's true intention through his many years of serving the Daishonin, faithfully and constantly.

---

54 **Four debts of gratitude:** Debt of gratitude owed to one's parents, all living beings, one's sovereign, and the three treasures.

Nikko Shonin recorded in writing the Daishonin's lectures as the *Orally Transmitted Teachings* (Ongi kuden).

With regard to this document, in *The History of the Fuji School* (Kechu-sho),[55] High Priest Nissei Shonin[56] wrote the following passage:

> After Nichiren Daishonin took up residence in Mount Minobu, he gave lectures on the Lotus Sutra in response to a request from his disciples. Although the Daishonin had a large number of disciples, he chose Nikko Shonin as his foremost disciple. Following the example of the Great Teacher Zhangan,[57] who documented the lectures on the Lotus Sutra and several other sutras given by the Great Teacher Tiantai, Nikko Shonin transcribed the Daishonin's lectures, which amounted to 229 articles. He compiled these articles together with other teachings that he heard whenever the Daishonin gave a lecture. This compilation is called the *Records Compiled by Nikko* (Nikko ki).
>
> (*Seiten*, p. 766)

---

55 *The History of the Fuji School* (Kechu-sho): A writing by the Seventeenth High Priest Nissei Shonin of Head Temple Taisekiji. It includes the achievements and biographies of the successive High Priests and other leading priests in the early period of Nichiren Shoshu.

56 Nissei Shonin [1600-1683]: The Seventeenth High Priest of Head Temple Taisekiji, who established the Nitemmon Gate and reconstructed the Mieido. After having heard Nissei Shonin's sermon, the future Twenty-sixth High Priest Nichikan Shonin entered the priesthood.

57 The Great Teacher Zhangan [561-632]: The second patriarch of the Tiantai sect in China. A disciple of the Great Teacher Tiantai. In order to hand down Tiantai's teachings to future generations, he transcribed and compiled Tiantai's lectures, which were later referred to as the three major writings—*Profound Meaning of the Lotus Sutra* (Hokke gengi), *Words and Phrases of the Lotus Sutra* (Hokke mongu), and *Great Concentration and Insight* (Maka shikan).

As indicated here, Nikko Shonin transcribed the important lectures on the Lotus Sutra that the Daishonin gave from the standpoint of the True Buddha. This document was reviewed and approved by the Daishonin.

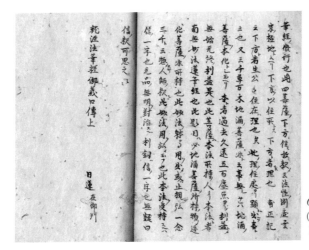

Orally Transmitted Teachings
(handwritten copy, stored at
Head Temple Taisekiji)

Following the same style as that of the *Orally Transmitted Teachings,* Mimbu Niko[58] also transcribed the Daishonin's lectures. That document is called the *Recorded Lectures* (Onko kikigaki) or the *Records Compiled by Niko* (Niko ki). Compared to the *Orally Transmitted Teachings,* this transcription does not fully describe the profound meaning hidden in the depths. It is, however, a valuable document that serves as a transcript of the Daishonin's lectures. Since ancient times, there has been a debate as to whether or not these two documents recorded identical lectures given by the Daishonin.

---

58 **Mimbu Niko [1253-1314]:** One of the six senior priests appointed by Nichiren Daishonin. Also called Sado-ko. After the Daishonin's passing, he misled Hakiri Sanenaga, the lord of the Minobu region, into committing many slanderous acts, and caused Nikko Shonin to leave Mount Minobu.

Toward the end of the *Orally Transmitted Teachings*, it says:

> The first day of the first month in the first year of Koan (1278)
> Written by Nikko
>
> (*Gosho*, p. 1815)

On the other hand, at the beginning of the *Recorded Lectures*, there is the following passage:

> A series of lectures [on the Lotus Sutra and its annotations] were given [by Nichiren Daishonin] from the nineteenth day of the third month of the first year of Koan (1278) to the twenty-eighth day of the fifth month of the third year of Koan (1280). Thus, I (Niko) have recorded these lectures in writing.
>
> (*Gosho*, p. 1818)

From this we can see that the *Orally Transmitted Teachings* is the compilation of lectures recorded prior to January first of the first year of Koan (1278). This means that it is a record of all the lectures completed by the end of the previous year. By contrast, the *Recorded Lectures* is the compilation of lectures given between March of the first year (1278) and May of the third year of Koan (1280).

Nichiren Daishonin giving a lecture

Regarding the contents, there is a marked difference between the two documents. It seems appropriate to conclude that the lectures themselves were different.

All things considered, it seems that the Daishonin gave lectures on the Lotus Sutra or its annotations two or three times at his dwelling in Mount Minobu. This is solely due to his great compassion to transmit the deep meaning of the true Law for the sake of his followers in his day as well as future generations.

Abutsu-bo and Sennichi ama (his wife)—Pilgrimages from Sado Island

There were two elderly believers from Sado who traveled all the way to Mount Minobu to visit the Daishonin in June of the eleventh year of Bunnei (1274). The Daishonin was so surprised to see them that he became almost speechless. They were Abutsu-bo and Ko nyudo, to whom he reluctantly bid farewell on Sado Island about three months earlier.

They had taken good care of the Daishonin, and when he left Sado, he thought that he never would see them again, since he had retreated deep into Mount Minobu. All he could do was worry about the old couples on Sado, with fond memories of them on the remote island. Because of this, he was overjoyed to see them, saying, "Is this a dream or an illusion?"

It seemed to have taken more than 20 days for Abutsu-bo and Ko nyudo to travel from Sado to Minobu. On their voyage, they took a great risk of being lost at sea, since they had to cross the raging Sea of Japan in a small boat. Moreover, if they had lost the opportunity to set sail on a clear day, they would have had to wait for days until the weather turned favorable. It was indeed a dangerous journey, with the constant threat of encountering pirates or bandits on their way. Especially, due to their advanced age, they needed an even stronger determination.

To them, however, the distance to Mount Minobu was nothing. Their desire to see and revere the Daishonin in person grew stronger and stronger each day. They became desperate to catch a glimpse of and serve the Daishonin even for a moment. Thus, they made a pilgrimage, single-mindedly yearning to see the Daishonin.

When they finally arrived at Minobu, the Daishonin gave them a sincere welcome. They certainly had a lively conversation with each other over the memories of their life on Sado. The Daishonin must have inquired about how Sennichi ama and Ko ama (the wife of Ko nyudo) were doing, since they were at home alone.

Abutsu-bo and Ko nyudo were filled with joy to have an audience with the Daishonin. Their prayer had been answered, dispelling all the hardships they had to undergo on their way.

The Daishonin wrote a letter to the wives of both Abutsu-bo and Ko nyudo, who continued to make tremendous efforts to see him. In his letter he not only praised Abutsu-bo and Ko nyudo for their determination, but also commended the firm faith of their wives, who had sent their precious husbands all the way to Minobu. He stated:

> You have sent your precious husband to me as your envoy. It seems like a dream or an illusion. I cannot see you, but I feel your heart certainly has reached here.
> (*Letter to Ko ama* [Ko ama gozen-gosho], *Gosho*, p. 740)

Abutsu-bo's second pilgrimage was around March of the 12th year of Bunnei (1275). The Daishonin wrote:

> I felt it was truly unexpected that Abutsu-bo visited me here in Kai Province, all the way from Sado Island. And how wondrous it was that he again visited me this year, and spent one month serving me by picking edible wild plants, bringing water from a river, and cutting trees for firewood, just as King Dan served the Seer Asita.
>
> (*Letter to Zenichi ama* [Zenichi ama-gosho], *Gosho*, p. 1220)

As this passage indicates, Abutsu-bo made another pilgrimage to Mount Minobu, and served the Daishonin for about one month. The Daishonin praised Abutsu-bo's sincere devotion and bestowed the Gohonzon upon him, saying that the good causes Abutsu-bo had made would also be definitely transferred to his wife, who had been supporting him in his Buddhist practices.

On July 27th in the first year of Koan (1278), Abutsu-bo, despite his old age of 90, visited Mount Minobu for the third time. In that year, an epidemic was spreading widely throughout Japan and a tremendous amount of people became ill and died, one after another. Since Abutsu-bo had not visited Minobu during the previous two years, the Daishonin was worried that Abutsu-bo might have been suffering from the disease. The moment the Daishonin saw Abutsu-bo, the first thing he asked was:

> How is your wife? How is Ko nyudo?
>
> (*Reply to Sennichi ama* [Sennichi ama gozen-gohenji], *Gosho*, p.1254)

Hearing that they were safe and had not been ill, the Daishonin was finally relieved. In the same Gosho, which was written on this occasion, he states:

> I have been here in the mountains of Minobu for five years, from the eleventh year of Bunnei (1274) until now, the first year of Koan (1278). During these years, you sent your husband [Abutsu-bo] three times, traveling from Sado to Minobu. How much faith you have! Your faith is firmer than the earth and deeper than the ocean.
>
> (*Gosho*, p. 1253)

The Daishonin praised Sennichi ama for her sincere faith. She had sent her elderly husband to visit the Daishonin three times during the five-year period after the Daishonin took up residence in Minobu.

For Abutsu-bo, who was 90 years old, in addition to the hardships he encountered on his way to Mount Minobu, he also had to constantly challenge his own physical limits. Therefore, each time he departed from Sado, he thought that this would be his last journey. He must have been overjoyed to meet the Daishonin these three times, and moreover, to be able to serve the Daishonin, leaving no regrets behind.

Abutsu-bo, then, passed away peacefully at the age of 91 on March 21st in the second year of Koan (1279). In the Gosho, *Reply to Sennichi ama*, the Daishonin stated:

> People are wondering where the spirit of the late Abutsu-bo has gone. When I look into the clear mirror of the Lotus Sutra for a reflection of his image, I, Nichiren, can see that he is facing east, inside the Treasure Tower of Taho Buddha at Eagle Peak.
>
> (*Gosho*, p. 1475)

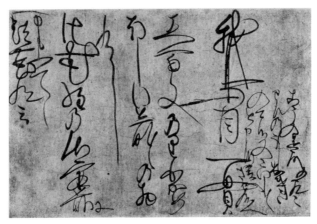

Reply to Sennichi ama (handwritten by Nichiren Daishonin)

This passage indicates that Nichiren Daishonin affirmed the enlightenment of Abutsu-bo. The Treasure Tower of Taho Buddha at Eagle Peak represents the Gohonzon, while Abutsu-bo being inside the Treasure Tower means that his life has entered and become one with the Gohonzon. Moreover, the Daishonin paid him the utmost respect by referring to him as "Abutsu shonin," which is an honorary title.

After Abutsu-bo's passing, his son, Tokuro Moritsuna,[59] followed in his footsteps, by visiting Mount Minobu and burying his father's ashes near the Daishonin's residence on July second in the same year. Twenty-three years later, Sennichi ama, Abutsu-bo's wife, passed away on August 14th in the first year of Kangen (1302).

Transcending time, as Nichiren Shoshu practitioners, this elderly couple teaches us the spirit of faith and practice and joyfully seeking the true Law. We can learn from Abutsu-bo, with his pure passion of

---

59 Tokuro Moritsuna [Dates of birth and death unknown]: A son of Abutsu-bo. After Abutsu-bo's death, Moritsuna visited Nichiren Daishonin in Mount Minobu and buried Abutsu-bo's ashes there. Following his father's will, he devoted himself to the propagation of the Daishonin's Buddhism on Sado Island.

yearning to serve the Daishonin as his disciple and visiting Minobu repeatedly from far away Sado Island, despite his advanced age. And we can learn from his wife, Sennichi ama, with her strong support for her husband by sending him off on a journey that might be dangerous and taking charge of the house during his absence. Their names will be mentioned eternally as model practitioners who show us the right attitude when we visit Head Temple Taisekiji and have an audience with the Dai-Gohonzon.

A great-grandson of Abutsu-bo, Nyojaku-bo Nichiman,[60] inherited the sincere faith of his great-grandparents, and constantly served Nikko Shonin as one of his disciples. Nikko Shonin eventually assigned him as the leading priest for the propagation of true Buddhism in the Hokurikudo (currently Hokuriku) region. Regarding this assignment *The History of the Fuji School* [Kechu-sho] states:

> The chief priest responsible for propagating the Lotus Sutra in the seven provinces of the Hokurikudo region...
>
> (*Seiten*, p. 698)

Nyojaku-bo Nichiman then devotedly propagated Nichiren Daishonin's Buddhism on Sado Island, his home.

---

60 **Nyojaku-bo Nichiman [Dates of birth and death unknown]:** A great-grandson of Abutsu-bo and a grandson of Tokuro Moritsuna. As a disciple of Nikko Shonin, he devotedly propagated Nichiren Daishonin's Buddhism and was appointed as "the chief priest responsible for propagating the Lotus Sutra in the seven provinces of the Hokurikudo region."

Mongol Invasion

In October of the 11th year of Bunnei (1274), five months after Nichiren Daishonin took up residence in Minobu, just as the Daishonin had predicted, a large army of over 25,000 Mongol warriors invaded Japan. This incident is known as the first Mongolian Invasion (Battle of Bunnei).

The Mongolian army landed on Tsushima Island on October fifth and on Iki Island on the 14th of the same month, and killed unarmed islanders there. Furthermore, on the 20th of the same month, the Mongolian army, gaining momentum, landed in the western area of Hakata Bay and advanced inland. Many commanders and soldiers, including the lord of Tsushima Province, and many local inhabitants died as a result of this invasion.

Nichiren Daishonin stated as follows:

> This is solely because of the people's erroneous views on Buddhism.
>
> (*Letter to Soya nyudo* [Soya nyudo dono-gosho],
> *Gosho*, p. 747)

He declared that the cause of these tragedies was due to the people's slandering the Law. He advocated that the government and the people of Japan should immediately renounce all the slanders against the Law prevalent throughout the country and take faith in true Buddhism.

Seven years later, in May of the fourth year of Koan (1281), the Mongols attacked Japan again with a vast army, even larger than the one sent during the Battle of Bunnei. This second attack is known as the Battle of Koan. Despite these two battles, the Mongols failed to invade the mainland of Japan. But these events eventually contributed to the weakening and fall of the Kamakura government many years later.

Atsuwara Persecution

In the 11th year of Bunnei (1274) after Nichiren Daishonin had entered Mount Minobu, Nikko Shonin carried out shakubuku activities in the provinces of Kai, Suruga and Izu. The propagation of the Daishonin's Buddhism dramatically advanced in the areas around Shijuku-in Temple in Kambara and Jissoji Temple in Iwamoto of Fuji County, where Nikko Shonin had received Buddhist training during his childhood.

Moreover, around the first year of Kenji (1275), Shimotsuke-bo Nisshu, Echigo-bo Nichiben, Sho-bo Nichizen[61] and others,

---

61 **Shimotsuke-bo Nisshu, Echigo-bo Nichiben, Sho-bo Nichizen:** Priests of Ryusenji Temple. They converted to Nichiren Daishonin's teaching through Nikko Shonin's propagation efforts. Nisshu was one of the six major disciples of Nikko Shonin and the founder of the Rikyobo. Nichiben was one of Nikko Shonin's disciples and the founder of the Renjobo. Nichizen was one of the six major disciples of Nikko Shonin and the founder of the Minaminobo. These three temples are among the lodging temples of Head Temple Taisekiji.

who belonged to Ryusenji Temple,[62] an old temple of the Tendai sect, converted to Nichiren Daishonin's Buddhism. This wave of shakubuku extended to the people in the neighboring regions. Three brothers, Jinshiro, Yagoro, and Yarokuro, who were trusted by the farmers of Atsuwara Village, also converted to the Daishonin's Buddhism. Subsequently, the number of new believers who took faith in true Buddhism continued to rise.

Fearing this situation, Gyochi,[63] the deputy chief priest of Ryusenji Temple, conspired with local government officials, supported by Hei-no saemon-no-jo, a top-ranking official of the Hojo clan at that time, and established a faction to fight against the Hokkeko believers in Atsuwara Village. Gyochi was looking for an opportunity to destroy them.

On September 21st of the second year of Koan (1279), many Hokkeko believers were helping to harvest the rice crop from Shimotsuke-bo Nisshu's fields. Hearing this, Gyochi hastily rounded up warriors who forced their way to the fields, where they attacked and wounded the farmers. 20 believers including Jinshiro were arrested there and held in custody at the regional government office in southern Fuji Province. They were accused of illegally harvesting the rice crop from a field owned by Ryusenji Temple.

Furthermore, Gyochi used the name of Yatoji (an older brother of Jinshiro and supposedly an officer of the manor of Ryusenji Temple), whom he had won over, and crafted a false complaint, in order to

---

62 Ryusenji Temple: A temple of the Tendai sect that was located in Atsuwara Village in Fuji County, Suruga Province (Currently Fuji City, Shizuoka Prefecture). On the premises where Ryusenji Temple of the Tendai sect once stood, the Sixty-sixth High Priest Nittatsu Shonin established Ryusenji Temple of Nichiren Shoshu.

63 Gyochi [Dates of birth and death unknown]: Hei-no sakon nyudo Gyochi. He was related to the Hojo clan, and is said to have been an evil priest who thought nothing of killing animals.

make Jinshiro and others appear to be criminals. Gyochi took further legal steps with the court in Kamakura. As a result, the farmers were transferred to Kamakura the same day.

Upon hearing this news, Nikko Shonin wasted no time to report the situation to the Daishonin in Minobu. Out of deep compassion for the believers in Atsuwara, the Daishonin immediately wrote a letter, which was later referred to as *On Persecutions Befalling the Buddha* (Shonin gonan ji), so that all his disciples and followers would be united and determined to overcome the adversity. At the same time, the Daishonin drafted the *Counterclaim against Ryusenji Temple* (Ryusenji moshijo), and Nikko Shonin wrote its final copy, which was presented to the court in Kamakura to explain what truly had happened.

On October 15th, when the *Counterclaim against Ryusenji Temple* was submitted, Hei-no saemon-no-jo, without clarifying the facts of the matter, interrogated the farmers at his residence. He threatened them by saying, "You must immediately renounce the Daimoku of the Lotus Sutra and, instead, chant the Nembutsu. Otherwise, you'll be convicted of a felony."

Jinshiro and the other believers, who were always taught to have firm faith in the Lotus Sutra, did not even wince and single-mindedly continued to chant Daimoku.

Hei-no saemon-no-jo was so infuriated at seeing the farmers chanting Daimoku, that he instructed his 13-year-old son, Iinuma hogan Sukemune, to torture them with whistling arrows. Despite this, the Hokkeko believers' faith did not waver at all, but rather, their voices became even louder as they continued to chant Daimoku. Hei-no saemon-no-jo exploded in anger, and finally beheaded three of them, Jinshiro, Yagoro, and Yarokuro, who were the leading figures among the farmers.

In this manner, during the Atsuwara Persecution, these farmers, who were in the weakest position in Japanese society, never gave in, refusing to renounce their faith. In particular, the three believers, who gave their lives for the sake of the Law, were later called "the Three Martyrs of Atsuwara,"[64] and have been praised as shining examples for the rest of the believers for generations to come.

Hei-no saemon-no-jo, who repeatedly persecuted the Daishonin during his lifetime, received severe karmic retribution for his actions, exactly as described in the Lotus Sutra. In the first year of Einin (1293), 14 years after he beheaded Jinshiro, Yagoro, and Yarokuro, Hei-no saemon-no-jo and his entire clan perished.

Nikko Shonin referred to this event in an inscription on the side of the Gohonzon that he transcribed on April eighth of the third year

---

[64] Right outside of the front gate of the Hoando, stands the monument of the Three Atsuwara Martyrs.

of Tokuji (1308). The inscription states:

> Fourteen years after (Hei-no) saemon nyudo (Yoritsuna) beheaded some of the Hokkeko believers (in Atsuwara), he was executed by the government on charges of plotting a rebellion against the Shogunate, and his offspring completely perished.[65]
>
> (*Essentials of the Fuji School* [Fuji-shugaku yoshu], vol. 8, p. 217)

The Monument of the Three Atsuwara Martyrs
at Head Temple Taisekiji

---

[65] This incident is known in Japanese history as the Revolt of Hei-no saemon-no-jo Yoritsuna (Taira-no-Yoritsuna).

The Dai-Gohonzon of the High Sanctuary of the Essential Teaching

Despite the fact that the Atsuwara farmers had taken faith in Nichiren Daishonin's Buddhism only for a short time, they continued to uphold the teaching in the face of such an unprecedented persecution. The Daishonin praised their strong faith and determined that the time had come to reveal the fundamental object of worship of the Buddhism of the sowing, for all mankind to uphold.

The Daishonin referred to the timing of accomplishing the objective of his advent in the following Gosho passage, written on October first:

> I first spoke about the doctrine [Nam-Myoho-Renge-Kyo] [at noon on the twenty-eighth day of the fourth month in the fifth year of Kencho (1253)]. Twenty-seven years have passed since then and it is currently the second year of Koan (1279). It took Shakyamuni Buddha forty-odd years, the Great Teacher Tiantai thirty-odd years, and the Great Teacher Dengyo[66] twenty-odd years to accomplish the purpose of their advents. The great and severe persecutions that befell them during those years are indescribable. I, Nichiren, already have discussed this matter with you. It has taken me twenty-seven years.
>
> (*On Persecutions Befalling the Buddha* [Shonin gonan ji], *Gosho*, p. 1396)

---

66 The Great Teacher Dengyo [762-822]: The founder of the Tendai sect in Japan, also called Saicho. He refuted Hinayana and provisional Mahayana Buddhism, which were prevalent in Japan, and dedicated himself to the propagation of the Lotus Sutra. He established in Japan the first high sanctuary of Mahayana Buddhism based on the theoretical teaching of the Lotus Sutra.

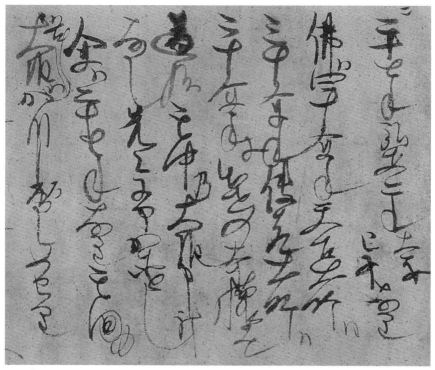

The passage quoted on the previous page from *On Persecutions Befalling the Buddha*;
handwriting of Nichiren Daishonin

In the midst of the Atsuwara Persecution, on October 12th of the second year of Koan (1279), the Daishonin inscribed the Dai-Gohonzon of the High Sanctuary of the Essential Teaching, accomplishing the ultimate purpose of his advent.

Considering the perpetuation of true Buddhism for eternity in the Latter Day of the Law, the Daishonin inscribed the Dai-Gohonzon on a thick wooden plank from a camphor tree. He then instructed his disciple, Nippo, to carve out the characters of the Dai-Gohonzon.

The Twenty-sixth High Priest Nichikan Shonin[67] expounded that the Dai-Gohonzon is the ultimate purpose of the Daishonin's advent. He stated:

> The Gohonzon of the High Sanctuary of the Essential Teaching, inscribed in the second year of Koan (1279), is the supreme entity of the Law of Nichiren Daishonin's entire life, and is the ultimate and conclusive purpose of his advent. It is the core of the Three Great Secret Laws, since it is, in fact, the original object of worship to save all living beings in the entire world.
>
> (*Exegesis on the True Object of Worship* [Kanjin no honzon-sho mondan], *Mondan*, p. 197)

---

67 **Nichikan Shonin [1665-1726]:** The Twenty-sixth High Priest of Head Temple Taisekiji. He was born in Maebashi, Kozuke Province (Currently known as Maebashi City, Gumma Prefecture). Before entering the priesthood, his secular name was Ito Ichinoshin. At the age of 19 in 1683, he heard a sermon given by the Seventeenth High Priest Nissei Shonin in Jozaiji Temple and decided to become a priest. He later, in fact, became a disciple of the Twenty-fourth High Priest Nichiei Shonin, and was given the priestly name, Kakushin Nichinyo. At the age of 44, he was promoted to the chief instructor of the Hosokusa Danrin Institute and his priestly name was changed to Kenju-in Nichikan. In March of 1718, he received the Heritage of the Law from the Twenty-fifth High Priest Nichiyu Shonin and became the Twenty-sixth High Priest of Head Temple Taisekiji. He organized Nichiren Shoshu doctrines by authoring the *Six-Volume Writings* (Rokkan-sho), the annotations of Nichiren Daishonin's Gosho and many more writings, thus promoting the truth and upholding the orthodoxy of Nichiren Daishonin's teachings. Furthermore, he devoted himself to the prosperity of Nichiren Shoshu by establishing the Ever-chanting Temple *(Joshodo)*. In addition, as one of the promoters he left the funds for building the Five-storied Pagoda *(Goju-no-to)*. Due to his great achievements, Nichikan Shonin is revered as a Restorer of Nichiren Shoshu together with the Ninth High Priest Nichiu Shonin. He passed away at the age of 62 on August 19th in 1726.

6. Nichiren Daishonin's Passing

The *Gotai-e* Ceremony, celebration of the eternal life of
Nichiren Daishonin, conducted at Head Temple Taisekiji
on November 20th, 2019

Document for Entrusting the Law that Nichiren Propagated throughout his Life (Nichiren ichigo guho fuzokusho)

In September of the fifth year of Koan (1282), the Daishonin chose Nikko Shonin among his disciples and bequeathed to him the Dai-Gohonzon of the High Sanctuary of the Essential Teaching. This means that the Daishonin put Nikko Shonin in charge of all of the Daishonin's disciples and lay believers after his passing and delegated to him the responsibility of leading the entire denomination in propagating the true Law.

As proof, the Daishonin transmitted the entirety of his teachings to Nikko Shonin through the following transfer document:

> I, Nichiren, transfer the entirety of the Law that I have propagated throughout my life to Byakuren Ajari Nikko and designate him the Great Master of Propagation of the Essential Teaching. When the sovereign embraces this Law, establish the [True] High Sanctuary of Hommonji Temple

at Mount Fuji. You must await the time. This is the actual precept of the Law.

Above all else, my disciples must obey this document.

The ninth month in the fifth year of Koan (1282)

Nichiren (signature mark)

The order of the Heritage of the Law: from Nichiren to Nikko

> (*Document for Entrusting the Law that Nichiren Propagated throughout his Life* [Nichiren ichigo guho fuzokusho], *Gosho*, p. 1675)

Before this transfer document was written, there was no specific mention of a place to establish the High Sanctuary of the Essential Teaching with the exception of *On the Three Great Secret Laws* (Sandai hiho-sho), in which the Daishonin referred to it as a supreme place that resembles the Eagle Peak of the pure land.

It was Nichiren Daishonin's will to establish the High Sanctuary of the Essential Teaching as specifically indicated in the *Document for Entrusting the Law that Nichiren Propagated throughout his Life*, which states, "establish the [True] High Sanctuary of Hommonji Temple at Mount Fuji."

The reason why the Daishonin transmitted the Lifeblood Heritage of the Law to Nikko Shonin is because among his many disciples, Nikko Shonin upheld absolute faith in the Daishonin and faithfully and constantly served the Daishonin based on the true master and disciple relationship. Furthermore, Nikko Shonin was outstanding among all the disciples in every aspect including his depth of understanding the Daishonin's Buddhism and his noble character. In order to propagate the doctrine down through the ages, exactly as taught by the Daishonin, based on the traditional standard of

Buddhism, the Daishonin selected only Nikko Shonin from among all his disciples and transferred his entire teachings solely to him.

Bushu Ikegami

The Daishonin, who had been ill in his later years, was urged by his disciples to go to Hitachi (present-day Iwaki City, Fukushima Prefecture) for recuperation in the hot springs. On September eighth in the fifth year of Koan (1282), the Daishonin left Minobu, escorted by Nikko Shonin and other disciples. On the 18th of the same month, en route, they arrived at the residence of the lord of Bushu Ikegami (present-day Ota Ward, Tokyo), Emon-no-taifu Munenaka.[68]

Starting on the 25th of the same month, at the Ikegami residence, the Daishonin gave lectures on the *Rissho ankoku-ron* (On Securing the Peace of the Land Through the Propagation of True Buddhism) to his disciples and lay believers. In these lectures, the Daishonin expressed his intention that all the disciples and lay believers should exert their utmost efforts toward the accomplishment of kosen-rufu with the spirit of "one's life is insignificant while the Law is supreme," and "you should be willing to give your life to propagate the Law." This is because the Daishonin's spirit of shakubuku is revealed in the *Rissho ankoku-ron*.

---

68 Emon-no-taifu Munenaka [Dates of birth and death unknown]: Ikegami emon-no-taifu Munenaka, whose younger brother was Ikegami Munenaga. They became believers of Nichiren Daishonin in 1256. Munenaka was disowned twice by his father, who was a strong supporter of Ryokan of Gokurakuji Temple. However, together with Munenaga, Munenaka finally led his father to take faith in the Daishonin's teaching. Nichiren Daishonin passed away at Ikegami Munenaka's residence in Ikegami (present-day Ikegami of Ota Ward in Tokyo).

Minobu-san Transfer Document (**Minobusan fuzokusho**)

On October eighth of the fifth year of Koan (1282), Nichiren Daishonin selected his six major disciples:[69] Nissho, Nichiro, Nikko, Niko, Nitcho, and Nichiji. After that, he bestowed upon his successor, Nikko Shonin, the two documents, *On the Transmission of the Seven Significant Teachings Regarding the Object of Worship* (Gohonzon shichika no sojo) and *The Transmission of the Heritage of the Law in the Hokke Hommon Sect* (Hokke hommon shu kechimyaku sojo ji, also known as *On the True Cause* [Honnin myo-sho]).

Furthermore, the Daishonin, feeling the time of his demise was approaching, appointed Nikko Shonin as the chief priest of Minobu-san Kuonji Temple. The Daishonin stated:

> I transfer Shakyamuni Buddha's teachings of fifty years to Byakuren Ajari Nikko. He is to be the chief priest of Minobu-san Kuonji Temple.[70] Laity or priests who disobey him will go against the Law.
>
> The thirteenth day of the tenth month in the fifth year of Koan (1282)
> Nichiren (signature mark)
> Ikegami, Bushu Province

---

69 Six major disciples: Six priests who were appointed by Nichiren Daishonin, later referred to as the six senior priests. From among them, only Nikko Shonin received the entirety of the Law. The other five priests disobeyed the Daishonin's will and refused to follow Nikko Shonin, the Daishonin's successor.

70 Minobu-san Kuonji Temple: A temple located in what is presently known as the Minobu Town in Minamikoma County, Yamanashi Prefecture. Nichiren Daishonin lived there for more than 8 years from 1274 to 1282.

(*Minobu-san Transfer Document* [Minobusan fuzokusho],
Gosho, p. 1675)

In the *Minobu-san Transfer Document* (Minobusan fuzokusho),
Nichiren Daishonin declared that he had transmitted the Heritage of
the Law, entrusted to a single person, to Nikko Shonin, and further,
he strictly admonished that any priest or lay believer who did not
follow Nikko Shonin would be going against and slandering the Law.

As stated in the *Document for Entrusting the Law that Nichiren
Propagated throughout his Life* (Nichiren ichigo guho fuzokusho),
Nikko Shonin received the transmission of the entirety of Nichiren
Daishonin's Buddhism, including the Dai-Gohonzon of the High
Sanctuary of the Essential Teaching, the origin of the Three Great
Secret Laws. Moreover, in the *Minobu-san Transfer Document*, the
Daishonin declared that Nikko Shonin was appointed as the leader
of all the priests and lay believers. These two transfer documents were
prepared by Nichiren Daishonin in order to clarify the position of
Nikko Shonin as the Great Master of Propagation of the Essential
Teaching, who had received the transmission of the Lifeblood
Heritage of the Law, entrusted to a single person.

The Passing of Nichiren Daishonin and his Funeral Ceremony

At the hour of the Dragon (approximately 8 a.m.) on October
13th of the fifth year of Koan (1282), at the age of 61, Nichiren
Daishonin, who had completed the transmission of his teachings
and guidance, peacefully passed away, as his disciples and believers
chanted Daimoku. It is said that at the time of the Daishonin's death,
the earth trembled and the cherry trees in the garden all blossomed

together, even though it was the beginning of winter.

There is a profound significance regarding the demise of the True Buddha, Nichiren Daishonin. It is the unfathomable Buddhist teaching that Nichiren Daishonin's life as the True Buddha eternally exists, while his physical body, which emerged as a common mortal in the Latter Day of the Law, is extinct.

On October 14th, the day after Nichiren Daishonin's passing, his body was placed in a coffin at the hour of the Dog (approximately 8 p.m.). Then, it was carried to the cremation ground by the funeral procession at the hour of the Rat (approximately 12 a.m.) and cremated there. The Daishonin's ashes were then placed in an urn. The entire funeral ceremony of Nichiren Daishonin was solemnly conducted.

Following the Daishonin's will, all aspects of Nichiren Daishonin's funeral were officiated by Nikko Shonin, the Great Master, who received the transmission of the Heritage of the Law, entrusted to a single person. Nikko Shonin, himself, recorded the proceedings of the Daishonin's funeral ceremony as *The Record of the Passing of our Founder* (Shuso gosenge kiroku).

Subsequent to the funeral of Nichiren Daishonin, Nikko Shonin officiated the memorial ceremony for the seventh-day after the

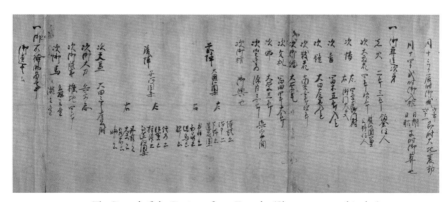

The Record of the Passing of our Founder (Shuso gosenge kiroku)

Daishonin's passing. Then Nikko Shonin, carrying the urn containing Nichiren Daishonin's ashes, left Ikegami in the early morning on October 21st, and returned to Mount Minobu on the 25th of the same month.

The Great Master of Propagation of the Essential Teaching

As the Great Master of Propagation of the Essential Teaching, Nikko Shonin protected the Dai-Gohonzon of the High Sanctuary of the Essential Teaching while taking a leadership role in all other temple-related matters, including the selection of the place where the Daishonin's urn should be enshrined.

After several years, however, Hakiri Sanenaga, the lord of Mount Minobu, began to commit various slanders, even though he had converted to the Daishonin's Buddhism and had begun his practice as a disciple of Nikko Shonin. He was deluded by one of the six senior priests, Mimbu Niko. In spite of Nikko Shonin's repeated warnings, Sanenaga never listened to him. Ultimately, he turned against Nikko Shonin.

At this point, Nikko Shonin came to the conclusion that the Daishonin's teaching would be tainted with slander if he continued to remain in Minobu.

In other words, he had no other choice but to leave Minobu in order to perpetuate the Daishonin's true teaching. Nikko Shonin quoted the Daishonin's will in *Reply to Mimasaka-bo* as follows:

> When the lord of Mount Minobu goes against the Law, I (Nichiren) will no longer reside in such a place.
> (*Reply to Mimasaka-bo* [Mimasaka bo-gohenji], *Seiten*, p. 555)

The Daishonin also made reference to the establishment of the High Sanctuary of Hommonji Temple at Mount Fuji. Therefore, Nikko Shonin finally made the decision to depart Minobu, based on the Daishonin's will.

Nikko Shonin expressed his thoughts as follows:

> Words cannot express the shame and self-reproach that I feel over leaving the mountain valley of Minobu. Having inherited the true Law directly from Nichiren Daishonin, I thought about this matter repeatedly. I came to be convinced that wherever I reside, what is most vital for me is to have the people throughout the world uphold it. Despite my efforts to persuade them, most of the Daishonin's disciples have turned their back on their master. I understand that only I, Nikko, am the person who upholds our master's correct teaching, and that I am the only one who will accomplish his ultimate purpose. I never forget his true intention.
>
> (*Reply to Hara* [Hara dono-gohenji], *Seiten*, p. 560)

For the sake of the perpetuation of the Law and kosen-rufu, with strong reluctance, Nikko Shonin left Mount Minobu with Nichimoku Shonin and other disciples in the spring of the second year of Sho-o (1289), taking the Dai-Gohonzon of the High Sanctuary of the Essential Teaching, the Daishonin's ashes, his Gosho writings, and all his other mementos.

Nanjo Tokimitsu,[71] the lord of Ueno Village in Fuji County, offered Nikko Shonin a field called Oishi-ga-hara, located at the foot of Mt. Fuji. Nikko Shonin built Taisekiji Temple on this land. The basis of Taisekiji Temple was established on October 12th, in the third year of Sho-o (1290). This laid the foundation for the

---

71 **Nanjo Tokimitsu** [1259-1332]: One of the influential believers during Nichiren Daishonin's lifetime. He was the lord of Ueno Village. His father was Nanjo Hyoe Shichiro, his mother was also known as Ueno ama, a daughter of Matsuno Rokuro saemon, and his elder sister was the mother of Nichimoku Shonin. He constantly made offerings to the Daishonin, and during the Atsuwara Persecution, played an important role under Nikko Shonin's direction. Because of his firm faith, he was referred to as "Ueno the Wise" and received many Gosho writings from the Daishonin, including *Many in Body, One in Mind* (Itai doshin ji) and *Reply to Ueno* (Ueno dono-gohenji). Later on, when Nikko Shonin left Mount Minobu, he invited Nikko Shonin to Ueno Village. He offered the land for Taisekiji and helped Nikko Shonin establish the Head Temple.

worldwide propagation of Nichiren Daishonin's Buddhism.

Thus, Taisekiji Temple was established on the ninth anniversary of the Daishonin's passing, when Nikko Shonin was 45 years old.

Since then, for more than 700 years, the light of Nichiren Daishonin's Buddhism has been passed down at Head Temple Taisekiji without any interruption, based on the Daishonin's will, as indicated in *On the Transmission of the Three Great Secret Laws* (Sandai hiho bonjo ji), and *Document for Entrusting the Law that Nichiren Propagated throughout his Life* (Nichiren ichigo guho fuzokusho).

Today, all Nichiren Shoshu priests and lay believers are advancing in unity toward the accomplishment of worldwide kosen-rufu and the salvation of all mankind for eternity.

Sammon Gate of Head Temple Taisekiji drawn circa 1910

Appendix I

Names of the *Samurai*

Samurai warriors in general bore a title following their sir name, as in the example of Ota saemon-no-jo ("Ota" is the sir name, while "saemon-no-jo" is the title). The title originally indicated one's military post assigned by the imperial court, and the samurais fulfilled their responsibility according to their title. However, it merely became a formality since many people during the Kamakura period chose their title as they preferred.

On the other hand, high-ranking officials of the Kamakura government, who were given a title by the imperial court, fulfilled their specific duties.

These officials and other samurais succeeded to and used their father's title in many cases. The following are examples:

- Saemon-no-jo (Saemon is also pronounced Zaemon)
- Emon-no-taifu
- Hyoe-sakan
- Kingo

Appendix II

Map of Japan

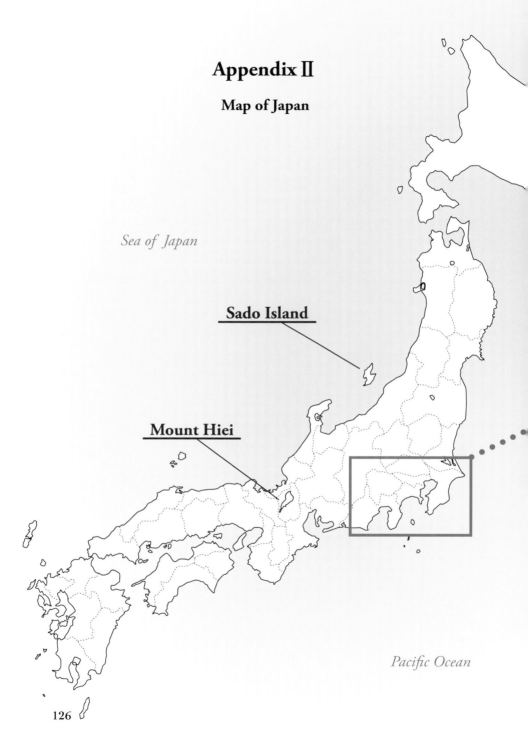

Sea of Japan

Sado Island

Mount Hiei

Pacific Ocean

Historical Locations Related to Nichiren Daishonin

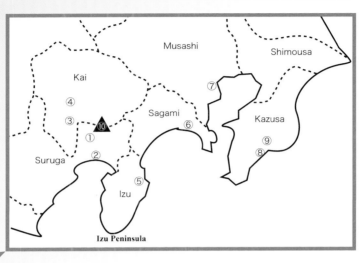

1. Head Temple Taisekiji
2. Atsuwara (Fuji City)
3. Minobu
4. Kajikazawa
5. Ito
6. Kamakura
7. Ikegami
8. Komatsubara (Kamogawa City)
9. Seichoji Temple
10. Mount Fuji

Appendix III

The Chronological Table of the Life of Nichiren Daishonin

	Year	Date	Age	Events
1221	3rd year of Jokyu	5/14	-	Jokyu Incident
1222	1st year of Jo-o	2/16	1	Born in Kataumi, located in Tojo Village in Nagasa County of Awa Province. He was named Zennichimaro at birth.
1233	1st year of Tempuku	Spring	12	Started his studies at Seichoji Temple in Kominato, Awa Province.
1237	3rd year of Katei	-	16	Entered the priesthood and changed his name to Zesho-bo Rencho.
1239	1st year of En-o	Spring	18	Set out on a journey to visit various temples in Japan for further studies.
1253	5th year of Kencho	3/28	32	Revealed the Daimoku of his inner realization at Seichoji Temple for the first time.
		4/28		Declared the establishment of true Buddhism at Seichoji Temple.
				Expelled from Seichoji Temple.
		-		Bestowed the precept of true Buddhism upon his parents, and changed his name to Nichiren.
		Around August		Built a hut in Matsubagayatsu in Nagoe, Kamakura, and began to propagate his teachings in Kamakura.
1257	1st year of Shoka	8/23	36	A major earthquake occurred in Kamakura.
1258	2nd year of Shoka	February	37	Perused all the sutras in the sutra storehouse of Jissoji Temple in Iwamoto of Suruga Province.
1260	1st year of Bunno	7/16	39	Wrote the *Rissho ankoku-ron* and submitted it to Hojo Tokiyori. Nichiren Daishonin's first remonstration with the nation.
		8/27		Matsubagayatsu Persecution
1261	1st year of Kocho	5/12	40	Exiled to Izu.
1263	3rd year of Kocho	2/22	42	Pardoned from the Izu exile, and returned to Kamakura.
1264	1st year of Bunnei	Autumn	43	Visited his mother in Awa Province and prayed for her recovery from an illness.
		11/11		Komatsubara Persecution
1268	5th year of Bunnei	January	47	An Official Letter from Mongolia was delivered to the Kamakura Government.
		4/5		Wrote *Rationale for the Submission of the Rissho ankoku-ron* (Ankokuron gokan-yurai) and submitted it to the Kamakura government, warning them that his prediction had come true.
		10/11		Sent remonstration letters to eleven high-ranking people in the Kamakura government and seven major temples.
1271	8th year of Bunnei	9/12	50	Assaulted and falsely arrested at his hut in Matsubagayatsu. At that time, remonstrated with Hei-no saemon-no-jo Yoritsuna. Nichiren Daishonin's second remonstration with the nation.
				Tatsunokuchi Persecution. Here, he discarded his provisional identity and revealed his true identity *(hosshaku kempon).*

	Year	Date	Age	Events
1271	8th year of Bunnei	10/10	50	Exiled to Sado Island
1272	9th year of Bunnei	1/16	51	Tsukahara Debate
		February		Wrote *The Opening of the Eyes* (Kaimoku-sho) in the Tsukahara Sammaido hut.
		Early Summer		Relocated from Tsukahara to Ichinosawa.
1273	10th year of Bunnei	4/25	52	Wrote *The True Object of Worship* (Kanjin no honzon-sho) in Ichinosawa.
1274	11th year of Bunnei	March	53	Pardoned from the exile to Sado Island, and returned to Kamakura.
		4/8		Remonstrated with Hei-no saemon-no-jo Yoritsuna again. Nichiren Daishonin's third remonstration with the nation.
		May		Entered Mount Minobu.
		After May		Nikko Shonin began to widely propagate Nichiren Daishonin's teachings in the provinces of Kai, Suruga, and Izu.
		10/5		Battle of Bunnei (the first Mongolian invasion of Japan)
1275	1st year of Kenji	6/10	54	Wrote *The Selection of the Time* (Senji-sho).
1276	2nd year of Kenji	7/21	55	Wrote *Repaying Debts of Gratitude* (Ho-on-sho).
1279	2nd year of Koan	9/21	58	Atsuwara Persecution
		10/12		Established the Dai-Gohonzon of the High Sanctuary of the Essential Teaching.
1281	4th year of Koan	5/21	60	Battle of Koan (the second Mongolian invasion of Japan)
1282	5th year of Koan	September	61	Gave the *Document for Entrusting the Law that Nichiren Propagated throughout his Life* (Nichiren ichigo guho fuzokusho) to Nikko Shonin and designated him as the Great Master of Propagation of the Essential Teaching.
				Departed Mount Minobu and arrived at Ikegami Munenaka's residence in Bushu Ikegami.
		10/8		Selected his six major disciples.
		10/13		Gave the *Minobu-san Transfer Document* (Minobusan fuzokusho) to Nikko Shonin and designated him as the chief priest of Minobu-san Kuonji Temple.
				Passed away at Ikegami Munenaka's residence at the hour of the dragon (around 8 a.m.).
1288	1st year of Sho-o	-	7 years after his demise	Nikko Shonin admonished Hakiri Sanenaga, who had been deluded by Mimbu Niko, due to the four kinds of slanders that Sanenaga had committed against Nichiren Daishonin's Buddhism.
1289	2nd year of Sho-o	Spring	8 years after his demise	Nikko Shonin left Mount Minobu.
1290	3rd year of Sho-o	10/12	9 years after his demise	Nikko Shonin established Taisekiji Temple, which is later officially called the Head Temple of Nichiren Shoshu, on the grounds called Oishi-ga-hara, which had been offered by Nanjo Tokimitsu.

英語　日蓮大聖人の御生涯

令和3年2月16日　初版発行

翻訳・編集　　宗祖日蓮大聖人御聖誕八百年慶祝記念局
発　　　行　　日蓮正宗宗務院

発　行　所　　株式会社　大日蓮出版
　　　　　　　静岡県富士宮市上条546番地の1

※本書を無断で転載・複製することを禁じます。

ISBN 974-4-905522-98-0